ICE OUT

CALUMET EDITIONS   AFTON PRESS

Minneapolis

First Edition February 2026
Ice Out: Minnesota Writers Rising Up.
Copyright © 2026 by Calumet Editions, LLC. All rights reserved.

10 9 8 7 6 5 4 3 2 1
ISBN: 978-1-962834-68-1

Cover art by an anonymous artist
Hand-drawn image of Minnesota by Kelly Frankenberg
Cover and book design by Gary Lindberg

Illustrations by Robin Schwartzman

To Renée Good, Alex Pretti, and all the individuals who at great personal risk protest ICE actions in Minnesota

ICE OUT

Minnesota Writers Rising Up

Prose and poems, edited with an Introduction by
Ian Graham Leask

CALUMET
EDITIONS   AFTON PRESS

Minneapolis

TABLE OF CONTENTS

IAN GRAHAM LEASK
Minnesota author and publisher

Introduction

I write this during a time of severe anxiety amongst the population of the most powerful country that has ever existed in human history, a country so divided in political opinion that it could potentially rip itself apart. Composing an introduction to a collection of short poetry and prose, all authored from one side of the political divide—liberals who count themselves as patriots, complaining about the behavior of conservatives who also count themselves as patriots—feels like a massive responsibility for someone who has always tried to be fair and see both sides of a dispute. I have written several versions of this introduction, none of which have done justice to the grave situation that I feel confronts the American people, and particularly the people of Minnesota whom I admire more than I can adequately express. I choose the side of kindness, empathy and the rule of law, and I know this is not good enough yet, but it must go to press.

Why the hurry? I'm an immigrant. No one except ICE sees me as such because I'm British, Caucasian, and retain a distinctive accent. Before the murders started, I had an exchange with a gaggle of ICE personnel early in the surge—they are billeted in a hotel across from my gym. The exchange wasn't overtly dangerous, but as punishment for my sarcasm about their rather swanky accommodation, they remarked with apology that because I sounded foreign, I should produce my identification. Smugly, I pulled out my US passport card and the incident ended with a *Have a nice day.* Suddenly, accents mean more than they should, I realized, and I went into a deep reverie about how easy that encounter was for me and how hard it must be for people with brown skin. I'm a lucky immigrant. How would I feel if armed men arrived at the door of my comfortable house, handcuffed me, and flew me off to some smelly detention center far from my loved ones? If this book helps to sway even one person's mind to prevent that from happening to another innocent immigrant, it will have been worth the effort.

I came to Minnesota decades ago, not to better my life but more in a quest to explore this extraordinary land. In my twenties, frustrated with British politics, I relocated to Saarbrücken, West Germany, where I had time to write, study, and learn a lot about the origins of National Socialism—Nazism. I worked as a meat porter in a *schlachthof* and taught English at night. I never thought of it as an act of emigration from the UK or immigration into Germany, but that's what it was. They gave me a grey cardboard *Arbeitserlaubnis*—with a photograph and fingerprint. My young wife at the time always felt "other" there, so we eventually moved to Minneapolis—her hometown—where, despite divorcing, I've resided ever since, much of the time with the status of a Permanent Resident, holding the so-called green card. I never felt vulnerable with that status until the Trump era.

I came to love Minnesota, and Minneapolis in particular, with its rich ethnic diversity and its reasonable and honest people—the best of whom are like friendly, easy-going Hobbits with a tinge of Canadian in their speech. Eventually, I took US citizenship because my roots had sunk deep into Minnesota and I wanted to vote against what I see as the dangerous ascendency of conservative extremism. I never lost my hunger for education and have always kept an open mind about politics. If one allows oneself to strip away the filters of religion, class, race and group affiliation, any sense of authoritarianism becomes anathema. Now, to my utter horror, I see all the signs of authoritarian governmental control emerging because of Donald Trump's draconian policies during the first year of his second term in office.

If you had read anything about *Project 2025*, a right-wing manifesto circulating before the last election, you knew what was threatened but probably didn't expect it to ever be implemented. Why would you? You live in America! But now we find ourselves invaded by masked Orcs, under the spell of their Dark Lord, with their fake mandate of doing the bidding of the American voter—getting rid of dangerous criminals and the rest of the Administration's obvious bold-face lies, all, in fact, to punish a state that in the last three election cycles has rejected the Trump agenda. All ICE agents do is arrest or kill white demonstrators and terrified immigrants, many of whom are green card holders or even citizens. It's brutal and not what we expect from a civilized nation. Their claim to have arrested great numbers of these so-called dangerous criminals needs objective verification and should be contrasted against the levels of criminality in other cities, particularly ones in "Red states." I like to ask evangelical Christians—the MAGA ones—what side they think Jesus would be on. Boy, do they get mad. They start quoting the Old Testament.

The ironic title of this book, *ICE OUT*, references a charming Minnesota idiom for springtime, meaning that the lakes, of which there are thousands, have thawed and we have open water. Time to plant fresh crops! The hilarious cover art represents the way Minnesotans have shown resistance against the brutality of poorly trained Federal "officers" with water balloons, silly string, car horns and whistles—which we hope will never escalate into violence. We found an unsigned image of such resistance on social media and couldn't resist using it on the cover. Whoever the artist is, we thank them for their brilliance and will credit them in a second edition, if there is one. It reminds us of "Braveheart" and depicts the ultimate defeat of a despot—Donald Trump's Bannockburn or Waterloo.

Instead of violence, which would've been understandable after the murders of Renée Good and Alex Pretti, and the abduction of infants, Minneapolitans have kept their cool, knowing better than to give the Trump administration a reason to declare martial law against a "Blue" city—one of the best in the Union. At the time of writing, claims of violence against ICE agents are utterly false.

We have assembled the unique skills of Afton Press and Calumet Editions, two Minneapolis publishers who share office space, to release this anthology of writings about the occupation of Minnesota by ICE agents and the tragedies that are unfolding as a result. We asked Minnesotans, particularly poets, to compose and donate short pieces of work, tailored specifically to this subject. This writing, composed within the crucible of the greatest threat to our freedom, may be the most important work ever in the pursuit of preserving democracy in the United States of America.

Not only will this project expose the appalling results of the decision by the Trump administration to violate the rights of American citizens and the human rights of non-citizens, but it will attempt to raise substantial funds for a full historical exposé to be published later by Afton Press, a 501 (c) (3) nonprofit publisher, specializing in Minnesota subjects. We have started the search for the right author to objectively research and write the most important of Minnesota books. Supporters can donate to general operations at www.aftonpress.com.

Why, in my own tiny way, have I taken on this monster? Because my dad taught me how to throw a right hook against school bullies. Because I read *The Hobbit* and *The Lord of the Rings*, *1984*, *Mein Kampf* and *The Rise and Fall of the Third Reich*, and because I made sure that I understood history and geography and science. Because I understand how civil wars start. I initiated this for my fellow Minnesotans—especially the writing community—and anyone in the world who insists upon freedom from tyranny. I'm too old to throw water balloons and stand in the tear gas, but I still have that right hook in me, transmuted into words—ones which represent the GOOD in the hearts of the best people in America!

ANONYMOUS
(from Eben Shapiro's Substack)

Minneapolis Diary

Wednesday, January 7

11:10 AM My partner texts me from work: "Looks like there was an ICE shooting over by (our friends' house). It's in the Strib." I pull up the Minnesota Star Tribune on my laptop. Both of our friends, who live at 34th and Portland, are quoted in the rapid-fire live news reports. They heard shots. They saw a woman getting CPR behind a snowbank. I text my friends to see if they're ok. They text back: "We are back inside trying to calm down." More live news reports roll in. The woman is dead. Stunned and horrified, I read eyewitness accounts and watch the video of Renee Good's murder. I'm glued to the news all day. An afternoon Zoom meeting with local clients peters out after about 20 minutes. One of the women needs to go home because she's concerned about an ICE incident happening at Roosevelt High School in her neighborhood. Another, who is normally cheerful and outgoing, can barely speak. Later, I watch Kristi Noem's press conference. *War is peace. Freedom is slavery. Ignorance is strength.* Is this really happening?

Thursday, January 8

The vigil for Renee Good continues on 34th and Portland. Thousands have come to pay their respects, to voice their pain and anger. I check in with our friends. They say: "It's like 2020 again, honestly ... but with the vigil right on our corner." In 2020, our neighborhood was on fire in the wake of George Floyd's murder. Helicopters begin to circle above. I have feelings of PTSD. Will our neighborhood go up in flames again? Or worse?

Friday, January 9

Weekly family movie night featuring a takeout meal. I read a post on NextDoor that urges support for a nearby beloved restaurant owned and operated by three Mexican sisters since 1996: "These ladies are scared and their business is slow. Please order take out and help them survive these times." We've eaten there many times. The sisters are very sweet women. I call to place an order. (They only take orders over the phone). I call again. And again. And again. No answer. Instead, I order from a Tex-Mex restaurant just down from the sisters' place on East Lake Street. When I go to the Tex-Mex place to pick up my order, taped to the front door is a message, handwritten in red Sharpie on cash register tape:

ICE
spotted
nearby
please
wait a
moment
and we
will let
you in.

I hope that the sisters are just scared. What an awful thing to have to hope for.

Saturday, January 10

I need to find some solace somewhere. I take a route that avoids traffic from the Powderhorn Park protest and go to a concert at a South Minneapolis church featuring a local folk duo I've never seen before. One woman plays cello, the other banjo and accordion. Their voices and harmonies are beautiful. As soon as they start singing, I burst into tears. I cry through much of the performance, especially during the canonical protest songs they have us all join in on. *Just like a tree that's standing by the water, we shall not be moved.* Afterwards, I tearfully thank one of the musicians, telling her I didn't realize how much I was carrying inside. We hug.

Sunday, January 11

Vicious attacks on both citizens and non-citizens in public places are happening every day, all over the Twin Cities. I watch numerous incidents unfold on video. One of the worst, filmed at a Speedway gas station just a few miles from my house, shows a young brown-skinned man being brutally dragged from his car by half a dozen masked men in camouflage gear, while Greg Bovino, flanked by six more agents, threatens observers with arrest. By the time the agents are done with the man, he's face down on the cold cement, unconscious.

Monday, January 12

10:20 AM I'm driving my teenage son to the YWCA to do his workout. As we cut through the Target parking lot, out of the corner of my eye, I think I see some commotion. I drop my son off and head back towards home. As I pass Target, I hear a cacophony of whistles and honking horns. I see a crowd forming. I pull into the parking lot, park,

3

and get out of my car. There are two parked SUVs with two ICE agents sitting inside each of them. A woman hands me a whistle. The group of maybe 10 of us blow our whistles. Some record video on their phones. Some take photos of the license plates. We are white, black, Hispanic, old, young. A Metro Mobility driver pulls up and honks his horn. The deep blaring of the horns of trucks making deliveries to Target and Cub adds to the sonic mix. We keep going for five minutes. The ICE agents drive to another spot in the parking lot. We follow them. Other people join. Some shout obscenities. Others say, "We don't want you here!" Finally, the ICE agents leave. One guy bangs on the side of one of the SUVs as they go. I wish he wouldn't. A Hispanic man touches me on the shoulder and says, "Thank you." On the way back to my car, I spot two young Minneapolis policemen getting into their vehicle to leave the scene. I tell them, "Thank you. We know you're not them." "Stay safe," they say.

Tuesday, January 13

Trump on Truth Social: FEAR NOT, GREAT PEOPLE OF MINNESOTA, THE DAY OF RECKONING & RETRIBUTION IS COMING!

Wednesday, January 14

It's been a week since Renéee Good was killed. ICE numbers continue to grow and their activity is escalating. Our mayor and governor continue to speak out against the military takeover of our city, asking ICE to leave so peace and safety can be restored. I read a lot of powerful, moving posts on NextDoor. People horrified by the increasing lawless violence going on in our community, offering to get food for those afraid to leave their homes, to drive their kids to school for them. There

4

are ugly posts, too. People cheering ICE on, celebrating their innocent neighbors being treated with unimaginable cruelty. I believe that there are more people with open eyes and hearts here than those without. But in Minneapolis right now, we are Ground Zero of Trump's America.

Thursday, January 15

Yesterday evening, in an address that succinctly sums up the horrors that have been going on here, Governor Walz called out the administration's "campaign of organized brutality" and told Minnesotans that Donald Trump wants more violence on our streets. "We cannot give him what he wants," he said, and instead asked protesters to peacefully record ICE agents' activities to amass a database of their tactics for possible future prosecutions. Within an hour, another person was shot in the leg by federal agents and the protest turned violent.

Trump on Truth Social: "If the corrupt politicians of Minnesota don't obey the law and stop the professional agitators and insurrectionists from attacking the Patriots of I.C.E., who are only trying to do their job, I will institute the INSURRECTION ACT, which many Presidents have done before me, and quickly put an end to the travesty that is taking place in that once great State. Thank you for you (sic) attention to this matter! President DJT"

Mayor Jacob Frey has called the ongoing situation with federal law enforcement "unsustainable." I'm not a religious person, but what's going through my mind right now is "God help us all."

ALAN DAVIS

Minnesota author of *Clouds Are The Mountains of the World,* which dramatizes how marauders and authoritarians disrupt the lives of residents.

Rampart Street

During WWII in New Orleans my mother's parents, who were Italian, were harassed violently; two agents barged into their house, ripped apart their furniture and terrorized them, with my mother, a youngster, as a witness.

My grandfather, frozen in his favorite chair, tried to negotiate but the agents left only after seeing their papers and putting the fear of God into them just because they were Italian and thus might have sympathy for Mussolini, even though they had left Sicily to get away from authoritarian Mafia goons who demanded tithes as a condition of doing business.

One of the agents, my mother said, called them dago trash who should go back to Italy. "I saw red," she said, "and screamed at them I don't know what. They thought it was funny and laughed, but my father sent me to my room after they left."

In Minneapolis, masked marauders executed two innocent U.S. citizens: Renee Nicole Good on January 7, and Alex Pretti on January 24. The 37-year-old mother was fatally shot by an ICE agent when she stopped to support her neighbors. ICE and/or CBP agents shot Pretti, a peaceful protestor holding a camera. ICE (Immigration and Customs Enforcement) and CBP (Customs and Border Protection) are distinct Department of Homeland Security agencies. They threw Pretti down after he assisted a woman who was pepper sprayed by masked ICE and CBP marauders; when a marauder found a pistol tucked under Pretti's jacket, they executed him.

Turns out Pretti had a permit to carry that pistol legally. He never brandished it. It was the masked marauders—ICE and CBP agents—who tore it from its holster, despite Pretti's second amendment rights, and used it as an excuse to kill him.

I thought the administration believed in the second amendment. Certainly, on January 6, 2021, many of their supporters showed up to protest Trump's election defeat toting all kinds of weapons. Of course, the Capitol police weren't masked, nor were they marauders. They were good, decent men and women.

Administrators like Stephen Miller and Kristi Noem, without evidence, told the American people not to believe our eyes, but undoctored video evidence is impossible to refute.

Pretti's parents responded: "We do not throw around the hero term lightly. However, his last thought and act was to protect a woman. The sickening lies told about our son by the administration are reprehensible and disgusting. Alex is clearly not holding a gun when attacked by Trump's murdering and cowardly ICE thugs."

My grandfather started a grocery store in New Orleans on then-bustling South Ramparts Street near Tremé. He had a green card but never became a citizen. I don't know why. He was an upstanding, taxpaying resident with an accent.

He had 13 children, all of them born in the United States. My mother was the youngest. They're all gone now. Two of her siblings were victims of Hurricane Katrina. The family history, that is, is the history of twentieth and early twenty-first century New Orleans. All of them were proud to be Americans.

Jenn Budd, in her memoir *Against The Wall: My Journey from Border Patrol Agent to Immigrant Rights Activist*, writes that "The pattern and practice down here [on the border] is to make false accusations against the people you just beat up." And then, she's told, "Deny. Deny. Deny. Counter-allegate. Deny."

Budd recounts how she was raped by a fellow ICE/CBP trainee and how her instructors did their best to make her feel it was her fault. They tried to shame her into quitting. She refused to back down. ICE/CBP culture's unspoken motto is, she tells us, *Do whatever you can get away with.*

Sound familiar? It's what those agents did to my mother's family. When one of my mother's brothers complained to local authorities, there was no record of the visit, he was told.

If my mother was alive, she would be disgusted to see and hear what's happened in Minneapolis and would call it out for what it is, a riot by agents working on behalf of an administration for which a dictatorial oligarchy is obviously a goal that's already been partially achieved. She was a law-abiding woman throughout her life, timid even, but she never lost her anger at authoritarian abuse; in fact, she passed it on to me. Sinclair Lewis published a novel titled *It Can't Happen Here*, but it happened here then and it's happening here now.

Ramparts Street was the "back of town," an historic and dilapidated border separating the French Quarter in New Orleans from Tremé. It's where my mother's family took a stand and held to their dignity, just as so many in Minneapolis refuse to back down.

In Moorhead, Minnesota, across the state and contiguous with Fargo, where there hasn't yet been an ICE surge, more than 350 people gathered on January 27 in a church to get training from the Immigrant Defense Network on how to be constitutional observers. "The training was one of 30 being sponsored by IDN as part of its "Brave of Us" tour across the Upper Midwest "to strengthen community readiness, solidarity and response." (*Fargo Forum*).

8

In Minneapolis, Governor Walz called up National Guard troops after Pretti's execution to protect protestors from ICE and CBP agents. And what did the Minnesota National Guard do, as opposed to ICE and CBP marauders? They handed out hot chocolate, donuts, and coffee to protestors and media. They wore reflective vests, not masks, and secured the safety and security of the protestors and media. That's how good law enforcement works.

The current administration's master plan is obvious: terrorize the population, ignore the Constitution and its Amendments, and enrich very rich business leaders (and themselves) at your expense and mine.

It's quite possible that Minneapolis (and Minnesota) is Trump's Waterloo, but that verdict won't be decided anytime soon. Instead of mistreating you, we give you hot chocolate, donuts, and coffee. We go after crooks and (most recently) fraudsters, not cooks.

To the best of our ability, we do our duty to the Constitution and to our neighbors, whoever they might be.

Hey, are you doing yours? Join us.

BECKY BOLING

Retired Spanish professor, poet, citizen, resident of Northfield, Minnesota

That Sleep of Death

They sleep under thermal blankets
in rented motel rooms, government-paid.
Thick curtains and blinds snuff out sunrise.
Dreams shout in their ears? Do they cringe
when windshields shatter. Pebbled glass
covers the bucket seats, scatters on the road.
When they batter down the door is it
their five-year-old child's face quivering
with fear that stares up at them, unable
to see their father behind the mask of shame?
Their nights cannot be restful—not if there's
any justice in this life, their stomachs filled
with pizza and free refills of soda at the parlor
where later that night they detained the staff
who prepared the meal and served them.
Do they think about the ones dragged out
of their jobs, their homes, their schools
and sent off to tent camps in a Texas desert?
Tears do not melt this ice. It is too thick,
a glacier's worth, so cold that it burns.
When they wake, are they surprised
to see their breath freeze into cloudy vapor,
to find the bathroom pipes have burst
and windows glazed in a foggy sheet of ice?

BEN KREILKAMP

US Army veteran 1969-71. He's made community theater in Minnesota since 1971.

Stepping into History

This is what democracy looks like.

This is what history feels like.

I'm learning how history feels. I've studied history in books both factual and fictional: Graves' *Goodbye to All That*, Woolf's *Mrs. Dalloway*, Nabokov's *Speak Memory*, Bolano's *By Night in Chile*, Fanon's *Wretched of the Earth*, portrayals of cataclysmic events in societies, Orwell's *1984*, Mandelstam's *Hope Against Hope*. Now I'm *experiencing* all that, learning how history feels when something seismic shifts. Overnight life feels different, everything changing at once. There's a sense of danger in the air: reports of masked men, armed, in the streets of my neighborhood. There is fear in the gym where I work out. Conversations are hushed as we worry who might be MAGA. It's clear our government, led by a deranged president, is terrorizing us, its citizens. A friend weeps on the phone telling me about the father with his little kids she took to a dentist appointment that morning: *Ben, they're so frightened*! We really have entered Ann Frank territory, neighbors helping neighbors. This is no movie. Time to step up.

I'm learning how to make choices. One does what one can. At 78 I carry a whistle but do little more. Going out on one of the bitter sub-zero days to deliver groceries, the ice was too slick for me to risk a fall, so I donated some cash to someone younger to do that work. A paradox arises among the fears and my limitations: a positive—learning to appreciate the communities here. I've never felt quite Minnesotan, certainly never proud of

11

my state, in spite of having lived here more than 50 years. I tend to see the negatives in its culture, but now...

And still more paradox: Facing the fear I'm feeling more alive, learning to let go of habit, to be kinder to my neighbors and strangers, learning to be thankful for my good luck. Smiling at strangers, they smile back, we share a secret: Aren't we lucky, right now, in this moment? The everyday moment of safety has become more precious. I think of Mandelstam's Russians in St. Petersburg, huddled in kitchens, sharing *samizdat* manuscripts that they memorize and then burn, always aware of the dangers of government spies in their midst.

Southside! Minneapolis is finding an identity, like the Maidan, or Stonewall, Tiananmen Square, Gettysburg, Waterloo, places famous for liberation won or lost. *Historic.* Our yard signs are weathered, sprung from years of ongoing struggle. Today these present battles amplify their old messages: AIM, Land Back, Black Lives Matter, Immigrants Welcome Here, Free Leonard, George Floyd: Never Forget, the Rainbow Flag. This land called Minnesota is being pressed into a new form by historic forces, stolen from the natives, mangled and poisoned by the profiteers, greedy corporations, lumber barons and Big Ag. People are rising up and forming new bonds, finding our voices, fresh communities among the wreckage. Anything is possible. A new day dawns. I've lived here more than fifty years and finally I feel *Minnesotan.*

BILL MEISSNER

Author of five books of poetry, four of short stories, and three novels

The Glass Breakers

Beware. They might approach your car any time:
In the early morning, during the long stretch of afternoon,
or out of the frightening silence of night.
They are the glass breakers.
They arrive suddenly with guns, with tear gas,
with blunt instruments,
their dull fatigues blending in so you can't
distinguish them from the grey shadows in an alley.
There are no laws for them. Anger is the only law they follow.
Power is their only god.
Do not try to speak to them. They have no use for words—
their mouths are sealed tightly under ash-colored masks.
They're idling right now in vehicles
on your neighborhood streetcorner, ready
to angle in front of your car
and block the path to your future.
So please beware. They're ready
to strut up to your driver's side window, anxious
to break through the glass, anxious
to send sharp icy pieces flying into your face,
blinding you like bullets, like tears.

BOB GILBERT

Former resident of Minneapolis and author of the political novel *A Firm State of Heart*

Viva la resistance!

Despite wintery temperatures, there's no lack of heat in Minnesota. Since their state was invaded by 2,800 federal agents, their people have been engaged in a passionate confrontation. You'll never convince them that this ICE operation is necessary or patriotic. The rhetoric that the feds are there to rid the community of criminals will never sell. They see the truth through the eyes of their martyrs: George Floyd, State Representative Melissa Hortman, State Senator John Hoffman and now, Renee Good and Alex Pretti. Perhaps Trump's assault on Minnesota was inevitable. The Land of Lakes embodies everything he hates: liberalism, a strong sense of justice and morality, multi-culturalism. He's working to replace those values with a bigoted rage to give a leg-up to white dolts whose sordid souls demand someone to hate. Perhaps Trump thought that Twin Cities residents were so "Minnesota Nice," that they'd turn away when their Hispanic and Somali neighbors were being kidnapped. Obviously, he was never told about the activist side of Minnesota politics that includes men like Gus Hall, Hubert Humphrey and Paul Wellstone. By turning armed agents loose against Minnesota residents, he is re-igniting an American civil war.

Trump's campaign is targeted specifically at communities that support the Democratic Party. He's trying, via violence, to break their resolve and make them bow to his authority. I don't envy the responsibility foisted upon the Twin Cities community. They're blowing the whistle on tyranny. They're contending with masked, Gestapo-like thugs who are taking their neighbors away. They are facing legal consequences. And yet, the situation reminds us of the First Minnesota Brigade at the Battle of Gettysburg in 1863. Two hundred and sixty-two Minnesotans charged the Confederates and not a man wavered. They turned the tide of that July 2nd battle. That tipped the scale of the war so that less than two years later, the Union won. Now the sons and daughters of the North Star State find themselves hurled "once more unto the breach." They're risking their lives by speaking truth to power. Viva la resistance!

2.

President Donald Trump's comments about Minnesota's Somali community being "garbage" came just in time for Christmas. Now his redneck rank and file can hate people they'll never meet, and who live in a state they'll never visit. Trump's racism stirs the soul and gladdens the heart of his faithful. It's that jolt of dopamine-inspired contempt his minions crave. But can it alleviate their pre-holiday tension? I'm sure Trump hopes so since they're marching to the winter solstice in a double darkness. One is the result of the earth's rotation. The other stems from alienation, economic uncertainty, higher prices for Christmas presents and health insurance premiums that are going to double. What to do? Break out the scapegoat playbook and attack Black-African immigrants. For me, Trump's insult is personal. I lived in Minneapolis for 28 years. I coached soccer teams that included Somali teens. I found them to be diligent, brave and eager to prove themselves on the playing field. I wrote for a community newspaper and did a feature article on the Dugsi Academy, a Saint Paul elementary school which serves as a steppingstone for Somali kids transitioning to the Land of Lakes culture. On the day I interviewed their principal, he must have hidden all the "garbage" because I saw none of it. The Somali community came to Minnesota in 1992 to escape civil war. They now number over 70,000.

15

Most are citizens and they're not going anywhere. Yet I can only imagine the fear they felt when Presidwwent Slump said he wanted them all out of the country. They're yet another targeted constituency deemed undesirable by the MAGA cult. Welcome aboard my Somali brothers and sisters! You're in good company.

3.

Yes, it's ridiculous, but true. In Donald Trump's America, the racist demagogue is a patriot. The January 6th insurrectionist is a patriot. The brown-nose broadcaster of Fox News is a patriot. The plutocrat is a patriot. The masked ICE agent is a patriot. The male chauvinist pig is a patriot. They're worming their way into the mainstream since in Donald Trump's America acquiescing to willful ignorance is patriotic. Orange makeup and the combover is patriotic. Book banning is patriotic. Lining your pockets with taxpayer money is patriotic. Owning the libs is patriotic. Jeopardizing the health care of 20 million Americans is patriotic. O come let the rednecks adore him. Let them throw out the baby with the bathwater. Let them straighten their red hats, put their hands to their hearts and sway to his siren song of fear and dread. Let them brag about their measureless qualities. Let them chant "hallelujah" from sea to shining sea. And yet, MAGA members are too shallow to realize how far they've gone astray. They've embraced the creepy underbelly of human behavior and sewed it into an ideology of greed and spite. White-boy rage fuels their movement. When their insults become cliched, when their rhetoric proves to be bad public policy, when their anger cools, as all anger will, they'll realize that they're headed to that place of shame: the American scrapheap of history. The growing opposition of open-minded, open-hearted Americans will never dumb down to their nonsense because they know that it's the cant of clowns and that it's truly unpatriotic

4.

Dominating the executive, legislative and the judicial branches of government is no longer enough for President Donald Trump. The demagogue and his sycophants have kidnapped American values and they're holding them for ransom. MAGA ideals are rooted in their much heralded, "Great Replacement Theory." A conspiracy is afoot to diminish the white population by immigrants, Jews, Muslims, people of color and globalists and it must be stopped! Their entire statecraft is based on it. Taken to extremes, it could yield dubious results. Can you imagine an entire NBA team of MAGA white boys? How will they feel when sportscasters call their on-court play "garbage" and on-line gamblers ignore them? MAGA only needs a few more Hispanics deported before they usurp Taco Tuesday. But how good will fried tortillas filled with Hamburger Helper taste to the palate? Should MAGA replace Jewish comedy with their own, will it be all belly and no laughs? Should they hijack haute couture from gay men, will western wear be the new fashion craze? MAGA values stem from a fear-based, dysfunctional psychology that's underwritten with lies. It's white supremacy on steroids. What's between us and them is no longer about politics, it's about morality. In his book, *Hillbilly Elegy*, Vice President J.D. Vance wrote that the poor, white working class is the most pessimistic class in society. He describes them as loveless, ever anxious and thirsting for outrageous stimulation. "They hate people who are different from them whether it's how they look, act or how they talk. Instead of engaging with the world they pull away. Feeling they have little control over their lives, they blame everybody but themselves." These are the people Trump is exalting in his great comb-over of American values. In their rivalry with rednecks, I'm proud to stand with those still brave enough to be American.

BRENDA E. MULRY

Saint Paul poet

Bullies

Bullies are aggressive,
intimidating, and coercive.
They dominate vulnerable people.
They lack empathy and guilt.

I thought I left bullies behind
from grade school,
from Junior high school,
and from Senior high school.

I thought I left bullies behind
when I quit working in schools,
where co-workers undermined me,
excluding me, taking unfair advantage.

I thought I left bullies behind
in my family,
where some family members
controlled and manipulated the narrative.

I thought I left bullies behind with bad friendships,
People who seemed like friends,
but really wanted to control everything,
What we discussed—usually about them.
What we did together—when it was convenient for them.

Now the bullies are here in Minnesota.
US Immigration and Customs Enforcement (ICE) agents
are everywhere, patrolling the streets.

They abduct immigrants and citizens
 -from their homes
 -from their workplace
 -from restaurants
 -from grocery stores
 -from schools
 -from daycare centers
 -from clinics.

They drive unmarked pickup trucks and SUVs.
They travel in packs.
You rarely see less than six of them together.

They wear masks.
They wear no identification.
They carry weapons:
-Glock 19 9mm pistols
-40 mm launchers,
-Stun guns (TASERS),
-Pepper ball launchers,
-Personal side arms, knives.

At least four or five agents surround a person,
throw them to the ground,
handcuff them,

and put them in an ICE vehicle.
If the suspect is lucky, they don't get beaten up or shot.

Two American citizens were not lucky.

A video shows, Renee Nicole Good,
the mother of three,
trying to drive away from agents.
She was shot in the left arm, right breast, head, and killed.

Alex Pretti, an ICU nurse and researcher
at the VA hospital, was killed yesterday.
He was protecting a protester from ICE violence,
while he videotaped ICE agents with his phone.

Alex was shot dead
once by one ICE agent
and at least nine more times by another
when he lay on the ground.

How do we stand up to these well-armed bullies?

From the onset,
we gather with neighbors
and our community,
to see what needs to be done and do it.

We do *Know-Your-Rights* seminars
and distribute leaflets.

We join training to be observers.
We write.

We volunteer and help our neighbors
with meals, groceries, rent, and supplies.
We volunteer and share funds for the needy,
We form a coalition for rent, food, and supplies.

We contact elected officials.
We form "a crowd, stay loud."
We use social media thoughtfully for factual material.
We volunteer and give visibility to groups engaged in immigrant defense.

We face the biggest bully of all in the president of the United States,
Donald Trump, who has started us on the road to fascism and dictatorship.
He has curtailed immigrants' rights, separated families,
destabilized communities and undermined our Democratic values.

His cabinet is corrupt and despicable.
The margins are narrow in the Senate and House.
The Department of Justice bows down to him.
We must resist the bullies.

We must believe that we will win.
Each of us has a role to play
in red states, in blue states,
and all political battlegrounds.

MAGA extremists seek to divide us
with absurd conspiracy theories to break our resolve.

Standing together is the only way
to protect our families, our friends,
our neighbors,
and our democracy.

BRITTANY KALLMAN ARNESON

Writer, singer and arts advocate living in Saint Paul, Minnesota.

During the Occupation, My Husband and I Tour a Preschool

I was already afraid.
Before children were snatched from school buses,
Before toxic gas filled the parking lots of daycares,
Before families huddled in the dark behind drawn blinds
Waiting for strangers to deliver diapers and groceries—
I was already afraid.
There were already so many threats in this place I call home.
So many unknowns. So many guns.
Too many for any parent's heart to hold.

And yet, it felt possible then to imagine
Sending my darling out into the world to make her way.
We had developed the necessary muscles required to
Raise children in this reality. Call it risk analysis, call it
Denial, call it just putting one foot in front of
Another, because time moves forward and kids grow up
whether you're ready or not.

Call it hope.

Call it what you will, we had it. We had done this once before—
Walked our baby to the bus stop in the pitch dark of so many early, frigid
Minnesota mornings, watched him, his little body almost invisible
    behind his backpack,
Climb the steps and pull away from the curb and into the future.

We knew the calculus of parenting, the constant negotiation between
Safety and opportunity, stability and growth,
Status quo and possibility.

Now, in this sweet school, I look past the rows of bright
Self-portraits, marching along the wall, their many colors
Mirrored in the faces of these tiny ones who follow their teacher
In a straight line like a row of baby ducklings. They glance up at us
Shyly, curiously. They are not afraid.

But I am afraid. I am looking past them, for the secure doors, for the signs
Prohibiting raids without a warrant. That is all I have—doors and
words—to
Place between my children and the armed men who would harm them
In the name of safety. That and my own body. And yet, my body
Cannot always be beside them. I have had to learn, alongside my children,
Although we once shared a body, we have now become distinct; we must,
At some point, separate.

And isn't this the oldest, deepest fear? The deepest
Dissonance, that we must surrender these fledglings, our most precious
Ones, these babies we birthed and bathed and
Breastfed? Our bodies are built to shield them from harm.
And yet, we know, even as we resist, even as we beg time to slow,
We know they will eventually (if we're lucky) grow
To where we can no longer hold them.

Eventually they must leave the nest. And we must let them.
And pray that, someday, if they find themselves in danger, some kind
Poet, some gentle nurse
Will show them mercy, will help them home.

BRUCE MORTON

Montana poet.

Winter in Minneapolis

They had it pretty and good
In Minneapolis.
But never again.
Even when the ice melts
And the hard chill abates.
The memory of this winter
Will be frozen in character
And place and people.
As if "nice" were not enough
To weather the bitterness
And harshness of the cold.
For this year it will not be
Denied that the climate has
Changed. But cold still kills.

BRUCE SPRINGSTEEN
Rights applied for.

Streets of Minneapolis

Through the winter's ice and cold
Down Nicollet Avenue
A city aflame fought fire and ice
'Neath an occupier's boots
King Trump's private army from the DHS
Guns belted to their coats
Came to Minneapolis to enforce the law
Or so their story goes

Against smoke and rubber bullets
By the dawn's early light
Citizens stood for justice
Their voices ringing through the night
And there were bloody footprints
Where mercy should have stood
And two dead left to die on snow-filled streets
Alex Pretti and Renee Good

Oh our Minneapolis, I hear your voice
Singing through the bloody mist
We'll take our stand for this land
And the stranger in our midst
Here in our home they killed and roamed
In the winter of '26

We'll remember the names of those who died
On the streets of Minneapolis
Trump's federal thugs beat up on
His face and his chest
Then we heard the gunshots
And Alex Pretti lay in the snow, dead
Their claim was self-defense, sir
Just don't believe your eyes
It's our blood and bones
And these whistles and phones
Against Miller and Noem's dirty lies

Oh our Minneapolis, I hear your voice
Crying through the bloody mist
We'll remember the names of those who died
On the streets of Minneapolis
Now they say they're here to uphold the law
But they trample on our rights
If your skin is black or brown my friend
You can be questioned or deported on sight
In chants of ICE out now
Our city's heart and soul persists
Through broken glass and bloody tears
On the streets of Minneapolis

Oh our Minneapolis, I hear your voice
Singing through the bloody mist
Here in our home they killed and roamed
In the winter of '26
We'll take our stand for this land

And the stranger in our midst
We'll remember the names of those who died
On the streets of Minneapolis
We'll remember the names of those who died
On the streets of Minneapolis

CAROL MARIE HEGRE

Minnesota senior citizen

I am a witness

I wasn't there
yet I see it a hundred times

It's in my brain
I can never not see it

It's over
but it's not over

Now they roam
They lurk
They grab and grasp and forever wound

Now I'm there
Silence
standing, looking
remembering again and again and again
No one speaks
the silence is unnerving
only the sound
of tires on the snow as a car slowly passes

Now here at this place
and the same quiet, slow motion of people moving
another circle
around candles and photos
posters, flags
memories
and flowers upon flowers
and flowers upon flowers

And now another place
from another time
but still here
but still remembered
still aching

I am a witness
etched in my brain
alive in my senses

Please, I can't breathe
I'm not mad at you dude
Are you okay?

I can never not be a witness

Is that all that I am?

CARY WATERMAN

Minnesota poet, author of *Threshold*

Birthday Poem

remembering Alex Pretti

On the morning of my grandson's 15th birthday,
just blocks from where he lives with his father,
a man is shot dead by ICE.
The man, Alex, is an ICU nurse at the VA.
He is shot ten times in the back
by two federal officers
as he lies on the frozen ground.
He was only an observer.

I hear all this on the news.
Then I call my grandson
and sing Happy Birthday to him.
Last night he had three friends sleep over.
They played games like Red Dead Redemption
and Geometry Dash.
They ate the pancakes my son fixed at 2 a.m.
then rolled out the blue sleeping bags.

They have gone home now,
picked up by nervous parents
on alert with car doors locked
because they never know when they might
drive down the wrong street

into the wrong neighborhood
where they could be stopped,
pulled out of the car
by mistake. Or not.
I tell my grandson not to go outside.
This is a war zone.
Not Gaza. Or Iran.
But Minneapolis.

Next year on this day
he will be Sweet 16.
He'll have his Driver's Permit.
He'll plan for college,
have a future,
what we hope for everyone's son.

CASS DALGLISH
Minneapolis resident, author and poet of *Ring of Lions*, 2025, and
Humming the Blues/ Cantando los Blues (a boca cerrada), 2026

Cold Enough

It's January here in the north and the snow's not over yet. We go for walks around frozen lakes and feed each other lines to help us survive. We ask our neighbors, "Is it cold enough for you?" and they tell us, "It could be worse."

And now it is.

Our streets are covered in ice that belches up from potholes, careens around corners, and pounds its way through front doors. Fragments of terror flash through the air and we swallow fear, but ice is on our breath when we speak of an old man thrown into the slush, of babies arrested, of a man fighting back with a snow shovel, a gun discharged in a mother's face, and a nurse shot over and over and over for helping a person in need.
Agents of power are tossing fictions like snowballs about what they've done, but we have been shooting movies while they were shooting guns, and we can see the truth. We are Minnesotans.

It's January. The snow's not over yet. The city lakes are covered in ice, but we all have boots and we can walk on frozen water.

A Lament for Minneapolis

From Humming the Blues/Cantando los Blues

(a boca cerrada)

Cass Dalglish, English

Catherine Rodriquez-Nieto, Spanish

Inspired by Enheduanna's Song to Inanna, 2350 BCE, Ancient Iraq

This was a city

there were terraces where people drank music from cups that burst with laughter and wisdom, but now memories come in splinters, like stars flashing through broken windows. Nothing is clear. The heavens withhold their light. This place has been abandoned. A smoky wind pushes death birds around... around... around. Is this pestilent flock our only deliverance? Listen. It's the voice of a child crying, but there are no mothers to give her comfort. No mother oil to be rubbed on her chalky lips, no mother water to quench her thirst, no mother ice to cool her, no mother fire to warm her, no mother path to accept the terror of her running feet. Only mother birds with mother talons, who call out their dirges from the sky and let them fall down to this godforgotten earth

Ésta era una ciudad

con terrazas donde la gente sorbía música de copas rebosantes de risas y sabiduría. Ahora, los recuerdos llegan hechos añicos, como estrellas que centellean a través de ventanas rotas. No hay claridad. Los cielos ocultan su luz. Éste es un lugar abandonado. Una humareda impulsa las aves de la muerte a dar vueltas... y vueltas... y vueltas. ¿Será esta bandada pestilente nuestra única liberación? Escucha. Es el llanto de una niña, pero no hay madres que la consuelen, ni aceite materno que suavice sus labios calcáreos, ni agua materna que sacie su sed, ni hielo materno que la refresque; ni fuego materno que le dé abrigo, ni sendero materno que acepte el terror de su huida. Sólo aves maternas con talones maternos que entonan sus cantos fúnebres desde el cielo y los dejan caer sobre esta tierra olvidada por los dioses.

CHRISTINE KALLMAN

Poet and playwright in Northfield, Minnesota, where she teaches aspiring musicians.

Lift Every Voice

Where is the music, my friend asked in November's chill
as a few of us waved our signs: No Kings!
and TACO! We longed to be swept up in a tsunami of sound
like in the 60s and 70s: "Give Peace a Chance"

and "Power to the People!" Did anyone
still know these songs? Who will write new songs
and who will lead them? Does anyone even care?
What could reach our hearts, shriveled and hardened

as they'd become, rattling around inside our little lives?
Then, in January, a mad president launched his goons
on Minnesota, sent them unreined, lawless, to terrorize, brutalize,
kidnap. To kill. Minnesota's hearts burst open

by the thousands, showing up in multitudes to march,
witness, speak the truth. Now we are feeding families,
transporting children, paying legal fees and rents. We kneel
and pray, we shout, we stand firm together. And, oh, there is music.

Not just Springsteen, but teachers and students, mothers
and fathers, grandparents, the Quakers, the Lutherans,
newly sprung justice-choirs surging with amateurs
and shining with row upon row of singers trained in beauty

and love on the choir risers of Minnesota schools, churches,
and town halls. Suddenly the crowds in the biting cold
are not just marchers, but near-heavenly throngs as their songs sanctify
the places Renee Good and Alex Pretti were gunned down.

All around, drums propel us. A voice rings out
and we echo in solidarity. There are old labor songs, new raps,
hymns, spirituals resounding on countless tongues the truth
that we shall not be moved, that in Minnesota

we believe in freedom and dignity for every human being.
That, even under the sinister shadow of hate and fascism,
we shall overcome.

D. E. GREEN

Poet and retired Augsburg English professor who lives in Northfield, Minnesota

Tengo miedo

I fear
the king.
He is
mad. He
rages
night and
day. His
henchmen
(and -women)
are killing
mothers
and poets
on the street.
Some folks,
our neighbors,
cannot leave
their homes
for fear
of being
dragged off
to prison,
deported
to some
Salvadoran

gulag run
by a crony
of the mad
king. They
shot Reneé
Nicole Good
for watching
them do
their evil
deeds. She
wrote poems.
She and her
wife have
three kids.
There were
teddy bears
in her glove
compartment.
They killed
her for no
good reason,
for no reason
at all. So
we are all
afraid. Still
we go out
into the icy
streets. Still
we whistle
warnings. Still
we shout
our "NO!"

DAVID LAWRENCE GRANT

Minneapolis-based screenwriter and playwright who also writes fiction and memoir.

One Single Voice

"Were you there last night?"

The "voice" rang as clearly in my ears as though someone very close by had spoken. But I have learned by now to discern the difference between a human voice and the vastly more subtle sound of a *thought* sent my way with supreme focus and intention. A sound is a physical thing, carried on sound waves through the air to the ear drums which vibrate to precisely the same frequencies which stimulate the neurons in the brain that process sound into what we perceive as noise, music, or language. But a *thought* is received like of flash of pure Spirit; instantaneous and nuanced.

I knew whose "voice" this was. My eyes scanned the top of the streetlight directly across from my front yard. There, I caught just a moment's glimmer of light from *his* eye, as my friend, a neighborhood crow, flew down to where I sat on my front stoop and stood a few feet away.

"Where?" I asked. "Was I where?"

"The place where all your tallest buildings sit."

"No. No, I've just gotten home from the hospital, the place they take us when we are very ill, or if something is broken."

Our friendship is deep and profound, so he went silent and turned slightly away, as crows will do when interacting with a human, to demonstrate a certain respect for our sense of privacy. They find our need for boundaries somewhat inscrutable and hard to understand, but they grant us the grace to be who we are. I knew he'd be far too polite to ask me *how*

I might be ill, or what in me might be broken. But I knew he wanted to know.

"This hip"…I pointed… "One of the joints that helps me stand and walk… it wore out, and they had to replace it with a man-made joint man-made. When a human gets to be 12 or 13 in crow years, these things can happen."

He seemed highly impressed that our technology can accomplish such things. But crows suffer no inferiority complex when they compare our technology to their own.

"We have no opposable thumbs," he once told me. "So, we worked with the intelligence and creativity with which we are gifted, and went on a long journey deep inside, where we have gained an understanding and mastery of many things. We live fully present where past, present and future are one. We have learned how to be anywhere… everywhere… nowhere… as we wish."

I do not pretend to be more than I am. I am no Shaman. I am as full of hubris, full of shit, and as mystified and terrified by this world as any other human alive. I possess no preternatural key—no astral Rosetta Stone—to decipher the language of any member of the animal kingdom I choose.

But I *do* understand Crow, an ability far harder-earned than anything I have ever learned to do – or most likely ever will. I make no claim to fluency, but I am learning. The most important thing to understand is that after years of attempting to decode their vocalizations, I made a momentous breakthrough that, when it came, hit me like a bolt of lightning: yes, crows make many kinds of vocalizations, but these represent only about five percent of their communication with each other.

Warnings, admonitions, expressions of extreme joy or grief, and the profligate, relentless stream of swearing they love to spew out into the world—*these* are all vocalized—with gusto. But most of their rich, profound language emerges as complete, complex thoughts to one another from what they call the Silence…from the spaces in between all the color and the noise of all that exists in this physical world.

This is a powerful, all-encompassing difference that completely separates the crows and their cousins, ravens, from all the others whom they consider to be mere *birds*.

"I'd almost given up on you," he once told me. "Most of us have no time for your kind… regard you, in fact, with complete indifference. You are among the creatures who grunt and squeal and squawk, allowing the entire universe of all the language you know to express itself through the sounds that spill out of your mouths. Yet you are the only ones among them all who have fashioned a way to record and preserve your words, creating great cathedrals of language that spiral out through the ethers, forever and ever, amen. You build marvelous things with your hands, but even so, your best trick is all that garbage you discard, It's the only thing most of us would miss about you if you were gone. Most of us, anyway. But those of us who *do* find you interesting, I have to say there is much about you that we admire. Like that night in the place where all your tallest buildings sit. We didn't see what sparked it, but we understood that your great gathering as a communal outpouring of anguish and grief."

"It was about standing together against injustice, but I couldn't make it. I was in hospital," I said. "I'm not sure I know how to express…"

"Cruelty. Callous, careless disregard for others… even unto death," he said.

I nodded.

"We felt you. Deeply. And anyone with eyes sharp enough to cut through the darkness would have seen scores of us up above you on the power lines and atop the lamp posts, rocking back and forth in solidarity with you. It's powerful when, in your thousands, you shout a thing, repeatedly, with one voice."

"I think so too," I said. "We call that chanting. It strengthens the connection between us…helps renew our faith in the principles for which we stand…our faith in each other and in ourselves. Makes us feel braver… stronger."

"But, to us, the most powerful kind of One Voice you do is the kind in which your voices blend in one vibration, for a long time…then another…then another. And when you land on these together, your voices caress each one the way those who deeply thirst caresses their first taste of water when it comes…from their parched tongues to the walls of their mouths, to their parched throats, all the way down into the bottom of their gullets."

"Singing," I said. "We call that singing."

"And then, sometimes, this leads to another kind of One Voice in which voices land on *different* vibrations, but still, they blend in a marvelous way. Makes us wonder if some of you have traveled to some of the same realms of light and sound where we have gone."

"Harmony," I said. "We call that harmony."

"Well, you will win the justice you seek," he said. "You will. Tell your friends and neighbors that we've seen it, and that we know you will not be denied."

We sat quietly for a long moment…listened to a pair of half-feral cats go at each other out back in the alley.

I quite forgot myself for a moment and reached out to stroke his feathers. That's the one place where crows maintain a boundary that's sacred and ironclad. No creature other than a crow is allowed to touch them in that way. He flinched and bristled, relaxed and let my hand linger there for just a beat, then flew off. I hoped my little misstep hadn't damaged our relationship. Moments later, he appeared by my side with a green ICE alert whistle in his beak. He dropped it against my new knee and flew away. He knew I felt bad about missing the protest. That's the kind of thing a real ride-or-die friend will do.

DEB DALE JONES
An independent scholar

hunting dogs

(or, love poem to South Minneapolis)

I was not born to be a hunting dog

that was clear enough from how well I did in school
in the post-Sputnik 60s, when girls were actually encouraged
and the whole community urging me on,
to get out, to make something of myself,
so I became yet another of South Dakota's biggest export —
      young people

a small town girl with rural, self-reliant values,
I wasn't prepared for the "Harvard of the Midwest"
(except, of course, academically)

after a couple of years I gave up on trying to figure out the Russo-Japanese war
      moved to South Minneapolis
      and started studying myself

I came into my own in Stevens Square
with its furnished efficiency apartments
      amid group homes
      drug addicts
      lonely pensioners

divorced men or divorcing
and professional volunteers

organizers and that little neighborhood newspaper
we were building community across difference

eventually I went back to school
and in a one-bedroom apartment on Powderhorn Park
I finished my Ph.D.

for me Powderhorn is the best of South Minneapolis,
especially on May Day with its parade and its puppets
and its pageant of overcoming winter yet again

not a hunting dog

I can't say I've made anything of myself
but I've muddled my way to a comfortable retirement
in a house in the suburbs with too big a yard
          and too small a garden

and frequent trips back to South Dakota
          where my mother still lives

not so much to South Minneapolis, especially not now
with so many Federal agents
who have too little training (or too much of the wrong kind)
and no memory whatsoever of that oath they swore
to uphold and defend the Constitution

that safe space is safe no longer

and no amount of study can help me understand
      the idea that shooting puppies
      is something to brag about
      something that could qualify you for a job

it makes me so sad
this imminent danger to our Republic
after two hundred and fifty years
in the vast expanse of history and pre-history
it is but a moment, shining with possibilities

no, we haven't ever gotten it right
this notion that all of us are created equal
no matter what kind of puppy we are

and I also can't understand
if you truly believe that God is our Creator
how you can defile that creation with so much destruction

we were none of us born to be hunting dogs

DIANE LeBLANC

Poet, author of *The Feast Delayed*

Guns and Candles

From anywhere else, we look like two kinds of people:
the ones with guns/the ones with candles.

But every morning is a call to wake and ask,
what are we doing with our guns and our candles?

Renee Good had no gun. But a voice and eye contact
were enough to get shot in Minneapolis.

Alex Pretti had a gun. Holstered and legal.
Enough to get shot in Minneapolis.

ICE agents have guns.
They are shooting Minneapolis.

The simpler the truth, the less I understand
but the more I believe we must resist.

After Saturday's rally in our town south of the city,
we rummage the cupboards for candles.

We're old, my husband and I, practiced at this
marching and lighting candles to remember.

Yes, it's somewhere near 20 below zero.
We drop our tealights in canning jars to keep them lit.

One by one, our neighbors emerge until small
flickers line our street in solidarity.

Someone is singing a hymn.
No one is pulling a trigger.

EUAN KERR

Retired journalist living in the Twin Cities.

At the intersection

A solitary figure stood on the median at a pedestrian-unfriendly intersection in the Minneapolis suburb of St. Louis Park.

It was the morning of Sunday January 25th, the day after ICE agents piled onto ICU nurse Alex Pretti, then shot him to death.

So bundled against the frigid cold was the human at the crossroad it was hard to tell if it was a man or a woman. The huge headphones hinted at youth.

The sign held overhead needed no interpretation: two words scrawled on a board attached to a piece of wood to facilitate waving.

Two words that mushroomed through the Twin Cities and elsewhere in the North Star State in previous weeks.

The first one is an expletive I try not to use. After making a living for decades using words, I know there are other better terms suited for difficult situations.

In this instance, it got the job done.

The second word is a staple of Minnesota descriptions: a source of humor in the face of climate reality.

But now it is the capitalized name of a brutalizing force imposed on a state which prides itself on welcoming immigrants.

It was just hours after thousands of Minnesotans lit candles and held vigils in wind-chilled parks and streets around the Twin Cities and the rest of Minnesota. Some sang. Many stood in agonized silence. All mourned Pretti and Renee Macklin Good.

The brave figure stood alone at the suburban intersection this Sunday morning. An individual moved to take action, to speak out.

Beneath the shock, the anger, the terror, and the sadness, the questions keep coming back.

How did it come to this? These sudden horrible events are the result of myriad actions and inactions over years and decades.

It's easy to point fingers, but deep down, do we not all carry a trace of complicity?

What twisted narrative resulted in a terrorized community and two violent deaths on the streets of a city which considered itself far from perfect, but at least striving to improve the lot of its citizens?

Two people just trying to help neighbors snuffed out in seconds by federal government agents.

How do we extricate ourselves from this nightmare? What is the exit strategy? For Minnesota? For the country?

How do we learn from what has happened and build for a better future?

How do we recover?

The bundled figure offered no answers, just raised the expletive sign and waved a gloved hand at the passing cars honking support in the bitter cold.

And finally, I felt hope.

FREDDY
An Immigrant in Minneapolis

Testament of Fear

Spanish

Hola, mi nombre es Freddy. Me moví a Minnesota hace 20 años buscando un futuro mejor para mi familia, y nunca me he movido de Minnesota; siempre he estado viviendo aquí. Este es un estado muy hermoso. Me encantan las personas de aquí: son muy amables y, a lo largo de estos años, he conocido a mucha gente.

He sido voluntario en mi comunidad de Richfield, trabajando con los niños, enseñándoles actividades deportivas y, sobre todo, a mantenerse activos.

Hoy en día estamos pasando por una situación muy difícil que nunca me imaginé que íbamos a pasar. El sufrimiento, la angustia y la incertidumbre de lo que nos pueda pasar es estresante. Estamos presos en nuestras propias viviendas, y nuestros hijos no pueden ni asistir a la escuela ni seguir con sus actividades diarias.

Gracias a nuestros amigos, podemos contar con comida y ayuda en nuestras casas, ya que no podemos salir a las tiendas porque inmigración está agrediendo mucho y tenemos mucho miedo, temor de salir de casa. Nunca pensé que iba a pasar esto en este hermoso estado.

English

Hello, my name is Freddy. I moved to Minnesota 20 years ago looking for a better future for my family, and I've never left Minnesota; I've always lived here. This is a beautiful state; I love the people here, they are very kind. Over the years, I've met many people. I've volunteered in my community of Richfield, working with children, teaching them sports activities and, above all, encouraging them to stay active. And today, we are going through a very difficult situation that I never imagined we would experience. The suffering, the anguish, and the uncertainty of what might happen to us is stressful, and we are trapped in our own homes. Our children can't even go to school or continue with their daily activities. Thanks to our friends, we have food and help at home since we can't go to the stores because immigration authorities are being very aggressive, and we are very afraid to leave the house. I never thought this would happen in this beautiful state.

GARY LINDBERG
Minnesota filmmaker, publisher and author of 16 books including
Seeing God in Many Mirrors

Ever-Present Guidance

A blizzard of opinions about the ICE siege of Minnesota swirls around residents and sometimes blinds us all to the fundamental issues on which humanity has received unanimous guidance from all our great wisdom traditions. Perhaps it is time to pause for a moment and recall the lessons handed down to us about the value of witness and truthfulness, the need for sanctuary and welcome, and the peril of raids and oppression. For those unfamiliar with this universal guidance, I offer the following concise anthology. You may be surprised at how our religions agree.

From Judaic Writings

Thou shalt not raise a false report. Put not thine hand with the wicked to be an unrighteous witness.

The Bible, Exodus 23:1 (ESV)

Thou shalt neither vex a stranger nor oppress him, for ye were strangers in the land of Egypt.

The Bible, Exodus 22:21 (KJV)

You shall not give up to his master a slave who has escaped from his master to you. He shall dwell with you, in your midst, in the place that he shall choose within one of your towns, wherever it suits him. You shall not wrong him.

The Bible, Deuteronomy 23:15,16 (ESV)

Learn to do good; seek justice, correct oppression; bring justice to the fatherless, plead the widow's cause.

The Bible, Isaiah: 1:17 (ESV)

Speak up for those who cannot speak for themselves, for the rights of all who are destitute. Speak up and judge fairly; defend the rights of the poor and needy.

The Bible, Proverbs 31:89

Thus saith the Lord, Execute ye judgment and righteousness, and deliver the oppressed from the hand of the oppressor, and vex not the stranger, the fatherless, nor the widow: do no violence, nor shed innocent blood in this place.

The Bible, Jeremiah 22:3

From Christian Writings

When the Apostles Peter and John were ordered not to speak of the miracles they had seen to prevent the truth from "spreading any further among the people," it is written that the Apostles said . . .

. . . we cannot help speaking about what we have seen and heard.

The Bible, Acts 4:17,20 (KJV)

Continue to remember those in prison as if you were together with them in prison, and those who are mistreated as if you yourselves were suffering.

The Bible, Hebrews 13:3 (NIV)

Blessed is the one who perseveres under trial because, having stood the test, that person will receive the crown of life that the Lord has promised to those who love him.

The Bible, James 1:12 (NIV)

We are hard pressed on every side, but not crushed; perplexed, but not in despair; persecuted, but not abandoned; struck down, but not destroyed.

The Bible, 2 Corinthians 4:8-9 (NIV)

Do not be overcome by evil, but overcome evil with good.

The Bible, Romans 12:21 (NIV)

Fear none of those things which thou shalt suffer. Behold, the devil shall cast some of you into prison, that ye may be tried, and ye shall have tribulation . . . Be thou faithful unto death, and I will give thee a crown of Life.

The Bible, Revelation 2:10 (NIV)

From Islamic Writings

Stand firm for justice as witnesses . . . If you distort the testimony or refuse to give it, then ˹know that˺ Allah is certainly All-Aware of what you do.

Qu'ran 4:135

If anyone... asks for your protection, grant it... then escort them to a place of safety.

Qu'ran 9:5

Do not enter any house other than your own until you have asked for permission and greeted its occupants. This is best for you . . .

Qu'ran 24:27

And do not conceal testimony, for whoever conceals it - his heart is indeed sinful, and Allah is Knowing of what you do.

Qu'ran 2:283

Do not let the hatred of a people lead you to injustice. Be just! That is closer to righteousness.

Qu'ran 5:8

From Hindu Writings

The Hindu Writings advise all to become one...

...who hates no creature, who is friendly and compassionate to all, who is free from attachment and egoism, balanced in pleasure and pain, and forgiving...

Bhagavad Gita, Chapter 12

May the guest be to thee a God ... you must follow only those virtuous actions which are irreproachable—and not others.

Taittiriya Upanishad – Siksha Valli

Never err from truth, never fall from duty...

Taittiriya Upanishad 1.11.1

The Writings list the virtues that one should acquire:

Harmlessness, truth, absence of anger, renunciation, peacefulness, absence of crookedness, compassion to beings, non-covetousness, gentleness, modesty, absence of fickleness...

Bhagavad Gita, Chapter 16

From Bahá'í Writings

It is not for him to pride himself who loveth his own country, but rather for him who loveth the whole world. The earth is but one country, and mankind its citizens.

Tablets of Bahá'u'lláh, Lawh-i-Maqsúd

The best beloved of all things in My sight is Justice; turn not away therefrom...

Bahá'u'lláh, *The Hidden Words* (Arabic)

Be a home for the stranger... a tower of strength for the fugitive.

Bahá'u'lláh, *Epistle to the Son of the Wolf*

Be anxiously concerned with the needs of the age ye live in, and center your deliberations on its exigencies and requirements.

Gleanings from the Writings of Bahá'u'lláh, CVI

Be in perfect unity. Never become angry with one another... Love the creatures for the sake of God and not for themselves. You will never become angry or impatient if you love them for the sake of God. Humanity is not perfect. There are imperfections in every human being, and you will always become unhappy if you look toward the people themselves. But if you look toward God, you will love them and be kind to them, for the world of God is the world of perfection and complete mercy.

'Abdu'l-Bahá, The Promulgation of Universal Peace

Ye are all the leaves of one tree and the drops of one ocean.

Tablets of Bahá'u'lláh, Bishárát

From Dakota Teachings (Mdewakanton / Lower Sioux)

To close a collection that has traced oppression through policy, raids through doorways, and silence through fear, it matters to end on a Minnesota truth older than the state itself: that the harm done to one life spreads outward—into families, communities, land, and water—and that repair begins by remembering our obligations to the whole web of relations. Agreeing that we "are all the leaves of one tree," a Dakota teaching names that responsibility with quiet force:

A commonly held worldview among us is Mitakuye Owasi (we are all related), *reflecting how all things, animate and inanimate, are intertwined.*

Minnesota Historical Society, Lower Sioux Agency:
"Dakota Makoċe (Dakota Homeland)"

GRETA LOU

A young, queer poet-organizer making home between unceded Dakota and Anishinaabe land (Minnesota), Abenaki land (Vermont), and Maya, Xinka, and Garífuna land (Guatemala).

For Renee Nicole Good

This year, the freeze came on fast. The snowstorms and
the windchills and the frostbitten branches. The breakups
and the letdowns and the violence—oh, the violence. It erupts
in summer heat or settles like sleet, for those who have it
monopolized first forgot to live the seasons. Their ancestors
rejected the lands that held their knowledge, ripped this one
from its relatives, outsourced labor to peoples without histories
of winter. Now they see those they would enslave making home
better than they ever learned. They enlist, respond with rage

while some of us relearn to notice. Flakes of tree bark,
translucent-thin beneath their scales. Fungus, big as human
hands protruding from softening trunks, or fine as hairs
filling decaying crevices. Every sliver of color: peeling lichen,
cascading needles, berries on spindle-bare bushes.
The half-full moon casting a halo of fog at first light.
Some of us are witnessing our fellow humans get
disappeared, and some of us are getting killed for it.

We thought there would be more time to prepare. We always
do, before the freeze. A thousand falls would not be enough
buildup and still, something in us was ready. We made whistles,

called neighbors, put picks on boots to walk the ice.
This is the story we've heard our whole lives. Told it, too.
They will try to kill you, our parents read to us. Your friend
or beloved will die. That will be when everyone starts to watch.

INGRID KONIECZNY

Special education teacher who lives in Northeast Minneapolis

The Real Monsters

Would you like to join our crew?
We pay really well
And we offer
Power

Are you emotionally stunted?
Terrible at having empathy for others?
Perfect
You're just what we need

Did you have a hard time as a kid
Parents not around enough
Maybe you were abused
Either way you felt a loss of control
That you've never
Quite been able to get back

We need people like you
Grasping for power
Anywhere you can find it
Insecurities hidden behind your
Bigotry and racism

Watch this quick training video and we'll
Pay you 50 grand
You'll get all the power you ever wanted
They'll have to listen to you now

Take your unresolved trauma
Out on others
Rip them from their families
You'll feel like the king of the world
Tear gas anyone who stands in your way
Even babies

The powers will be so strong
You won't know what to do with
The adrenaline
Rushing through your veins
A better high
Than the meth
Your dad was on when you were little

So good you'll almost be able to
Outrun your own demons
By becoming a demon
A monster
That everyone is afraid of

That'll show 'em
You've finally made it

At night when you try and close your eyes
Just use the money to plug your ears
To block out the sounds of the screams
You've caused
Eventually
It will become
A lullaby
To you

ISADORA GRUYE

Twin Cities poet and photographer

How to talk to your mom about ICE

January 7, 2026

Momma, they're shooting poets in the streets again
in bright morning light, in front of gathered crowds.
They're seizing teachers as class dismisses.
They're taking whole families from their houses,
handcuffing toddlers in the middle of the night.

When you were a teenager,
you rode your bike down these same streets -
on your way to volunteer for Bobby Kennedy.
You sang along to Dylan and Baez.
You learned to make your own clothes
instead of giving your money to an economy
that fueled the Vietnam War machine.

I know this isn't the world you wanted for me.
This isn't the world I want either.

Momma, the woman they killed this morning was a poet.
That scares you, because I'm a poet as well.
It was easy to see her blood in the snow as mine.

You don't want me to go to the protests
because they'll shoot me too.

I give you a hug and remind you –
this isn't the world I want either.

My life seems so small and quick,
when stacked against the bigness of the future.
And that future is worth the fight.

JASON TERRES

Minnesota poet

Minnesota salts the sidewalk

The soft wisps of soul slowly twist
In the bitter January air.
Neighbors flood the street
Carrying songs of solidarity
Whistling warnings of fascists among us
Coming to terrorize communities.
Unease stretches like an alleycat
Scarred, cold, and confused upon
How murder can be justified.
The frigid air traps treason.
All voices quiver in the cold
Yet Minnesotans still call out
Bold declarations of freedom
Of love for our neighbors.
Minnesotans are used to the chill.
We have mastered the ability
To maintain our smiles
Despite deplorable temperatures
And despicable temperaments.
We still gather on streets
Even after the white, pure snow
Has become worn and soiled
We again call out for justice.
This is a community too warm
Too used to helping each other salt the sidewalks

Of lending a hand,
Whether the pavement is slippery or not.
We know the sting of winter,
Yet still shrill shouts can call out
Proclaim roaring hearts persist
Burn bigger beat by beat
The furnace to melt ICE

JEFF JOHNSON

Minneapolis writer and editor

Trumperick du Jour, January 18, 2026

I Am Simultaneously the Greatest
King History Has Ever Known and the
Most Adorable Arctic Seal Ever Clubbed
to Death by Antifa Psychopaths

I'm Jupiter, phalanxed with moons.
I'm Moby Dick scorning harpoons.
      I'm Rosemary's baby!
      No mortal can slay me—
Except, once they've routed my goons,

Minnesotans with water balloons.

JOHN ROCHE

Poet in Albuquerque, New Mexico

Lament for the Twin Cities

2,000 federal agents sent to Minneapolis area to carry out largest immigration operation ever, ICE says.

—PBS 6 Jan 2026

Beirut
Fallujah
Ramallah
Crimea

This is what occupation sounds like:

"We are in charge here. You must comply."
"Your papers, please."
"Do not interfere!"
"Stand back!"
"Over there!"
"Hands on your head!"

Always the same male swagger
always the same smirk, masked or not
always arbitrary justice
at the end of a gun

Oh! Minneapolis Oh! St. Paul
We sat down by your mighty River
one June morn
and listened to St. Anthony Falls

We strolled your parks and museums
took the Green Line to Union Station on its very first day
gazed from the observation deck of the Foshay Tower
and at night from the 12th floor roof of a downtown building
watched the lawn bowlers on the roof of Brit's Pub
got drenched from a sudden shower on Nicollet Mall

We fondly recall your intelligent, friendly, cultured people
and your unhurried pace

But today we remember Melissa and Mark Hortman
Today we remember George Floyd and Philando Castile
Today we remember Renee Nicole Good

JOHN TUTHILL
Former resident of Minnesota

Sage wisdom from Rome

I reside in Rome, Italy, so I see the news in Minnesota through shit-stained glasses. Through the eyes of the media, the murder of Renee Good appears to be as significant as the murder of Archduke Ferdinand in 1914, an assassination which sparked WWI. Chatter on the right side of the pond envisioned the violence in Minnesota as the catalyst for WWIII and American Civil War II. I called my brother who lives in St. Paul near the Mississippi River. He told me that the media over-hypes the situation, so he is carrying on normally. I am not so sure of that. In Davos, Switzerland, Donald Trump, in front of God, Lady Gaga, his goons, and the global audience at the World Economic Forum, slammed Minnesota.

He said, "And ICE gets beaten by stupid people, by leadership in Minnesota."

Then he spit and drooled again by spouting this shit:

"The situation in Minnesota reminds us that the west cannot mass import foreign cultures when have never built a successful society of their own. We're taking people from Somalia. And Somalia is a failed, it's not a nation. Got no government. Got no police. Got no military, Got no nothing."

Minnesota has to use creative methods to defeat ICE. Fortunately, Minnesota is getting assistance from God by providing a round of 30-below weather. I presume many of these ICE mercenaries are from the South and struggle with the frigid weather.

Trump employed shenanigans with Scottish people regarding his golf courses. He angered many. Minnesota should recruit some of the meanest Scottish motherfuckers as bouncers in bars that employ foreign workers. They will receive a case of beer for every ICE officer that goes sideways out the door, slides on the ice and gets hit by an MTC bus.

Then, a local insurgent should go to the hotel where ICE is staying. Many of the ICE officers usually eat at the hotel restaurant so the insurgent can instruct the cooks to add laxatives to the food ordered by ICE.

Insurgents can impersonate an ICE officer using a fake southern accent, which would create dissent among the ranks. An example would be real ICE officers in a state of consternation when they see fake ICE officers marching with the protesters.

Pour water over their vehicles which would flash freeze in 30 seconds making it impossible for them to open the doors, windows, trunk, and hood.

Have the snowplows pile up snow around their vehicles so they cannot move.

Put a potato in the tailpipe of an ICE vehicle which would block exhaust flow causing a back pressure that would stall the engine and leak stinky fumes into the cabin.

Consult the Animal Human Society and find the meanest dogs and train them to attack ICE officers.

Invite ICE officers to run the Hypothermic Half Marathon in shorts.

When the ICE officers are having a meeting or a gathering at a restaurant, and have the Minnesota Wild hockey team along with the Winnipeg Jets arrive in full uniforms, and body-check them.

Just kidding. Sort of.

JULIE A. RYAN

Minnesota poet, essayist, novelist, and visual artist

Icy Sea of Vitriol

The invasion of winter and all its arctic blasts have come
to the Land of 10,000 Lakes. Will it last? Will it get worse?
Probably. Who knows? What will it look like before it goes away?

Like blizzards of polarizing persuasion to expose faces
that aren't snow white, to cage babies, to terrorize, to deport
citizens cursed by abhorrent obsessions of Cult Leader Trump;

the occupation of his frosty minions on a flurry of missions
to dump democracy, to sink everything good with weighted words,
to slice concerned voices with furies of icy bullets.

America's passionate activists, with their fiery opinions, will die
trying to swim across the current evangelical sea
of vitriolic brainwashing; they can't escape the glaze unhurt.

Yet, free-thinkers will keep diving in—visionaries, poets, nurses
floating images and words that might someday carve
soulless icebergs into more compassionate shores.

Heartfelt goals of someday welcoming those who dream
into sunny arms of opportunity will be ice-blocked by bigotry
that breaks even the buoyant wings of our better angels.

Still, benevolent spirits in urgent search of kinder ways
will continue submerging themselves well into the chilling brine
of this country's fascist marrow to embody resistance,

to assist in moving society past this present climate
through a just lens—live videos and poetic pens freezing moments
in time for future scrutiny, the unpredictability tyrants despise.

Those who dare own loving and merciful minds
will continue declaring a mutiny on self-righteous cruelty,
speaking truth until it cracks frigid perversions of power,

until the frozen ink, the stolen peace, and the silenced screams
are understood, until collectively sunken efforts stack up
to tower over the soulfully corrupt and finally build

that someday bridge to better days, to warmer ways—
a country free for all, a deprogrammed country free of icy vitriol
that stands on moral ground for good.

KELLY FRANKENBERG
Minnesotan, poet, artist

Casualties of Peace

The ground is slippery like the politics.
As frozen as their hearts.
We need solid ground to stand upon-
Understand upon.

Black. Brown. Indigenous. Human.
Immigrant. Neighbor. Citizen. Human.
White. Lesbian. Mother. Human.
Whistle. Protest. Peaceful. Legal.

Spray. Gun. Handcuffs. Imprisoned.

Stop! Go!

Stop! Go!

Gas. Brake. Gas.

Bang! Bang! Bang!

Shame!

Child. Alone. Orphan.

HUMAN.

It could have been me.
That could have been me.
That could have been me.
Then it was.
It was us all.
Death of humanity in 3 shots.

Terrorist. Blame. Shame.

Shame!

Justice for Renee Good!

But justice can only come
When humanity returns.

And through this horrendous injustice
We still stand with whistles.
We still stand with humanity,
So, to the world it's understood,
Why Minnesota Nice
Is now
Minnesota Good.

KILA KNIGHT

Received her MFA from Oklahoma State University. Her poems have appeared in *If You Can Hear This: Poems in Protest of an American Inauguration*, *orangepeel literary magazine*, and *The Poeming Pigeon*.

They want us to say nothing is happening here?

After "Dans l'Antre du Roi de la Montagne, Edvard Grieg" by Chen Jiang-Hong

Stroking sun onto canvas in my office as if I know how to paint. I'm trying to be creative, trying to reset after watching the news. An accidental contour and I am shaping the sun into a man's chest, pectorals bifurcated by sternum. I brush pigment from his face, think he looks like my windshield when I wash it with a gas station squeegee, when the dust that has been accumulating for weeks is finally allowed a respite. I've added dimension, conjured a god, check my phone.

My friend in Minneapolis sent me another video and a fresh poem. He was tear-gassed again; I hear him coughing from behind his camera as fumes billow, obscuring stoplights, buildings, and civilians. If one could just close their eyes and their ears, they could almost pretend they bore witness to a dust storm, or a wall cloud. Is this what they want us to say, that nothing is happening here? I type a reply, grip the paintbrush.

Splattering black on the surface, the pigment binds like slick blood. A third dimension: wet on wet crosshatching, undecipherable calligraphy, scattered downy barbs. I introduce green for balance, scrape black onto the god's chin, across his collarbone. A half-formed butterfly—an abrasion, formed from the flesh of his entry wound—emerges from his left oblique.

My friend messages:
strangers offered a hot meal,
rinsed his eyes with milk.

LAURA PACKER

Twin Cities writer and storyteller.

Nothing Unusual

Today, just outside of Minneapolis.

I stopped at a local Mexican place for lunch. I'm trying to support immigrant businesses. The door was locked and the sign read, "We Are Open, Please Wait." I knocked and waited, and soon I was let in. There was another sign in the foyer that explicitly stated ICE is not allowed in without a warrant. None of this is unusual now.

I placed my to-go order and settled at the counter to wait. The woman who let me in came over to ask if I wanted water while I waited, then saw my whistle around my neck. She looked me in the eyes. I smiled a little and said, "I'm so sorry about what's happening. I hope your family is okay."

There's no point in asking if they are safe. They are not.

She smiled a little at me. This is what she said.

"My son is 11 and he keeps asking me why this is happening. I told him he has to take his passport with him everywhere, and he needs to memorize his social security number. He keeps saying, 'Why, Mom? We didn't do anything wrong.' I don't know what to tell him.

"My husband has a business. All the guys who work with him, they're all Mexican, some citizens, but all legal. We're Mexican and we're American too. He offered to close for a week so they could stay home and stay safe, but they all said they need the money, they want to work.

"One guy, A, he has a wife and a little baby. ICE took him. He was walking from the store to his car and they got him. They took him at eight a.m. and by 1 p.m. he was in Texas. We don't know what to do to help him. We talked to a lawyer, but...

"He's here legally. He had his green card and his work papers. He kept telling them that he had those things, trying to show them, and they kept saying working papers don't mean he can live here.

"We talked to him a couple of times, we can't find him anymore. He told us last time we talked that they get one meal a day and one cup of water a day. Now we can't find him.

"— gave us a big box of diapers and food for the baby, but his wife, she's so scared. She doesn't know what to do. I don't either.

"Anyway, all of the guys still need to work because they all have wives and babies, but what if they get arrested? I don't know what to do."

We looked at each other, and I didn't know what to say. "I'm sorry" is pretty weak. We talked a little more, and when I paid my bill, I gave her all of the cash in my wallet (I'm paying with cash wherever I can because it's more durable in value than credit). She thanked me. I wished her luck. She thanked me for doing the things I'm doing.

I told her I would pray for A, his family, and hers. And I left. Because what else could I do? None of this is unusual now.

LOREN NIEMI

Minnesota spoken word artist and author of *A Breviary for the Lost*

Have You Not Learned?

ICE said that,
more than once
in a dozen variants
and while we're fearful
of their casual aggression,
it seems they have not
learned anything about
winter (may they slip
on their asses a thousand
thousand times).
What it does and how it
tempers us…

They will learn our dark
resolve under Minnesota
Nice – how we learned from
George Floyd the cost
of flames and that when
we stand together
we push back and yes, when
we push back in January
we are wearing our
ice cleats and mittens.
We will live here long after
these snowflakes depart.

On Circumstance

As a child I wondered what it would be like to live in Nazi Germany.
The movies made it seem like everyone was scared,
sneaking around, talking in whispers, and I suppose they were.

Now I know what it is to live in an occupied city.
Looking for the unmarked car speeding past at every stop sign,
Nervous as a tinted window SUV without plates approaches.

Sirens in the distance, the helicopters circling again,
Every trip to the grocery store is measured for risk,
Every phone call comes with the question, is anyone listening?

LORI A. BROWNING

Former Minneapolis resident, now living in Arizona, and author of the forthcoming historical-fiction trilogy *Brave New Atlantis*, inspired by early American experiments in social contract.

A Mirror in Minnesota

"It is excellent to have a giant's strength; but it is tyrannous to use it like a giant." —Shakespeare, *Measure for Measure*

You are not the enemy. Not the conservative neighbor who worries about disorder. Not the liberal neighbor who worries about cruelty. Not the working parent trying to keep a family afloat. Not the veteran who loves this flag. Not the immigrant who loves what this flag once promised.

The enemy is colder: *the slow training of a free people to accept what free people should never accept*—fear made into policy, dehumanization disguised as "security," and power that refuses accountability.

Minnesota is living in the crosswinds of it now. When federal enforcement feels like an occupation—when the street becomes a place where ordinary people hesitate, where a routine stop can become a disappearance, and a mother spends the night calling precincts and hospitals, hearing "we don't have that name" until dawn turns panic into a new kind of normal—something sacred is being tested: not party loyalty, but the American creed that power answers to law.

And this is no longer abstract. In January, Minneapolitans watched two residents die in separate encounters involving federal immigration agents—Renee Nicole Good on January 7 and ICU nurse Alex Pretti on January 24—while video and witness accounts contradicted the government's kneejerk initial story of what happened. Then came another jolt:

a 5-year-old detained by immigration agents at his Minnesota preschool, now held with his father far from home. And when official statements contradict what people can see with their own eyes, trust collapses—and fear rushes in to fill the gap.

This is why "Mirrors for Princes" mattered. Writers once held up a mirror to rulers and said: *If you are legitimate, you welcome standards. You accept restraint. You prove authority by mercy and justice—not by your ability to terrify.*

So here is the mirror, held up in daylight:

> If authority is righteous, it does not need shadows.
> If authority is lawful, it does not fear identification.
> If authority serves the public, it does not treat the public like prey.

Whatever you believe about immigration—however strongly you feel about borders and laws—due process is the line that makes us America. The Fifth Amendment does not say "citizen." It says: *person.*

If you can be persuaded that some persons do not deserve due process, you have accepted a fatal idea: that rights are not rights at all—they are privileges granted by power. And once rights become privileges, the only question left is: *who loses them next?*

We've also been sorted into teams with labels too crude to contain a human soul. We're taught to flinch at words instead of asking what they mean—until neighbors flinch at one another instead of at the erosion of law.

How did we become this divided? Part of the answer is propaganda—and I don't say that to insult anyone. I say it because it happened to me. I once believed my channel was the honest one, until a headline cracked something open and I saw it: bias isn't only what is said; it's what is never allowed to be seen. Omission creates a world where your side is always pure and the other side is always monstrous. That is how a decent person becomes certain—and certainty becomes permission.

So here is one concrete act of courage, especially for those who are afraid: step outside the algorithm. Taste more than one version of the world. Borrow a wider sky. Then choose—not your team—but your conscience.

And do the hard thing without becoming what you oppose:

> Do not be violent.
> Do not burn your city.
> Show up. Speak. Call. Witness.

This is not softness. This is strength. Because in every era, tyranny depends on the same resource: *the silence of the decent.* Boethius wrote *The Consolation of Philosophy* in prison while awaiting execution, and his counsel is quiet steel: *leave hope and fear aside.* Not because hope is bad—but because fear is how power trains good people into spectators.

So here are the non-negotiables. Not left. Not right. American:

- No hiding identity during public enforcement (clear agency + visible ID).
- Nonmarked "grab-and-go" tactics that resemble kidnapping to bystanders.
- No chokeholds / neck restraints—especially not on kids.
- No seizing children at schools or childcare without transparent, verifiable identification and immediate access for parents/ attorneys to locate them.
- No entering homes without proper warrants.
- No detaining people incommunicado—families and attorneys must be able to locate someone quickly.
- De-escalation and accountability must be standard, not optional.
- And the military is not a domestic police force.

If power is legitimate, it must stand in the light. And if it will not stand in the light, it is not protecting America. A country that tolerates secret policing is rehearsing for tyranny.

You are not the enemy. But if we allow fear to make us cruel, if we allow power to operate without accountability, if we allow "law enforcement" to become lawless, then we will wake up one day and realize we saved a slogan and lost a country.

A giant's strength is not the problem. The problem is when we let it move among the people without remorse. Because when that becomes normal, it doesn't matter what "side" you're on—the giant eventually steps on everyone.

LYNETTE REINI-GRANDELL

Resident of Portland Avenue, Minneapolis, and author of the memoir *Wild Things: A Trans Glam Punk Rock Love Story* and two collections of poetry.

To Be Present

is to hear the constant doppler blare of horns
bent tones driving past
the whistle shriek of warning in my mouth
as I try to fathom why.
All these ICE trucks, no road salt staining them,
too clean for Minnesota winters,
they don't fit, nothing fits,
their officers don't wear gloves,
anyone can see they don't belong here.
None of this belongs here.

Yet the traffic of the ordinary people
still creeps by and still I try
to figure out what all the soldiers
and their vehicles are doing in the middle
of my street, on Portland Avenue,
where someone walks her aging dog.

I cannot find a locus for their action,
as I wonder whose house they might break into
because that is what they've done before,
they break, they enter, grab, and they abduct
people, they take them their airport oubliette.

They even send the children to this dark machine,
I am thinking, when I hear a woman scream,
No, No, No, No...

Now I am screaming too because I have heard
the gunshots and all my air is rushing out of me
and I turn to see her crashed car, smoke billowing
from the engine
my lungs are breaking with the shock
and I am screaming and I am summoning
all my wraithish wrath to curse them,
shame them, name their crime, to somehow
send them back, they don't belong here,
what did you do what did
you do what
did
you
do
shame
shame
you shot someone
shame

And then
they will not let us go to her
they will not let us help her
we don't yet know Renée has died.

They want us to do nothing nothing nothing
and nothing keeps us from our mission now

to eradicate their evil occupation,
their cancer on our streets
to name the monster's origins
to send it back
to where it came from.

All we have of truth is witness
the evidence of so many
the recordings all of us have had to make
as we lean against each other for support,
as we create a buddy system,
we check in,
we watch warily each shiny SUV
and we stand on all the street corners
by the schools and wave at fellow watchers
to let them know that we're here for them too
even as they're here for us and all who need
our presence.

Hold on, hold on, hold on...
To be present. To stand together
for all in our community,
to take care of all
our community.

MARY K CRAWFORD-LORFINK

Author of historically-rooted, faith-inflected stories

Dear Time

Once I played in my mother's garden,
inhaling the fragrance of blush pink roses.
Sunlight filled our small patch of lawn.
The door was left unlatched.
Neighbors knew neighbors.
We were mostly refugees from Eastern Europe—
attending nearby city churches,
speaking the same foreign language.
Our mothers lingered over coffee,
sharing recipes and inviting conversation.
Six decades later, I am a different person.
I sync my life to weather and traffic.
My husband works his IT magic from our home office.
The doors are locked.
The house wired for security.
Every window bolted shut.
Drapes drawn.
Around the neighborhood,
on small squares of iced grass,
sticks with heavy cardboard signs
poke the lawns.
The signs watch us.
They lean into shame and doubt,
rage against the times.

I pause along the sidewalk,
somewhere between now
and the years to come.
"Let's Make America Great Again."
"Do better."
Still, no answers.
Emotions fade.
I pray for new dreams.
I've held out hope—
but who's in charge here,
and what do you mean
it's up to me?
Too many ghosts live around me.
The blue sky drops low to the earth,
a veil reminding us
the future is hidden from us all.
To ease my loneliness
and fear of what lies ahead,
I carry the sky—
no answers,
only breath.
The roses have faded.
Time does not turn back.
I stand here still,
listening
for what comes next.

MASSOUD AMIN

An executive, professor emeritus, and author of the forthcoming book: *The Integrity Compass: Leading with Ethics in a Changing World*

As an Immigrant, I See a National Threat

I never imagined that in my adopted home of Minnesota, I would witness American citizens shot dead by federal agents on our streets. Yet in the span of a few short weeks, two Americans—a 37-year-old ICU nurse and a mother of three—have been killed during US Immigration and Customs Enforcement (ICE) operations in Minneapolis. As an immigrant who came here believing in the promise of liberty and justice, I am alarmed. This is not simply a Minnesota tragedy; it is an American crisis. The threat unfolding here is national in scope, and it strikes at the heart of what America stands for.

American Lives Lost in an ICE Crackdown

On January 7, 2026, Renée Good—a US citizen, poet, and mother of three—was fatally shot by an ICE agent in Minneapolis during a chaotic immigration enforcement action. Just over two weeks later, on January 24, federal agents opened fire on Alex Pretti, a 37-year-old intensive care nurse at the VA hospital, killing him in the middle of a city street. Both were U.S. citizens killed on their own city streets. Their deaths occurred during a surge of federal immigration agents deployed to Minnesota under orders from Washington—a campaign that officials claim is about enforcing immigration law, but which ended up spilling the blood of the very people the government is meant to protect.

These killings have shaken our community. Eyewitness videos and reports clearly prove that neither Good nor Pretti posed a lethal threat when they were gunned down. Pretti, by all accounts, was attempting to help fellow community members and was holding a phone, not a weapon, when agents tackled and pepper-sprayed him. Good was trying to drive away from a tense scene when an agent fired into her vehicle, striking her three times, killing her. In both cases, the response by federal officers was disproportionate and deadly. This was not supposed to happen in America—not in the nation that prides itself on the rule of law and the sanctity of life.

A Constitutional Crisis Unfolding in Minnesota

What followed these deaths has only deepened the alarm. Instead of transparency and accountability, we have seen obfuscation and power struggles. Federal officials immediately spun narratives painting the victims as dangerous criminals – with one official, Greg Bovino, outrageously claiming Pretti intended to "massacre law enforcement" and calling him a "would-be assassin", accusations that eyewitness evidence flatly contradicts. Minnesota's governor, Tim Walz, bluntly described the claims from Homeland Security Secretary Kristi Noem and senior agent Bovino as "lies."

Even more disturbing, the US Department of Justice moved to block local investigations. Minnesota's state investigators were prevented from accessing key evidence in these shootings; several federal prosecutors resigned rather than target the victims' families as instructed. State authorities had to sue the federal government to preserve evidence from the scene of Pretti's death—a judge had to order DHS not to destroy or alter anything. In Congress, alarmed legislators are accusing the administration of "efforts to avoid accountability" for potentially violating citizens' constitutional rights under color of law. In other words, officials fear that the very government charged with upholding the law may be breaking it, then covering it up.

This crisis hits multiple pillars of American democracy:

- The right to life and safety: Unarmed Americans have been killed by federal agents on US soil, a shocking overreach of force.
- The rule of law: Federal authorities have stymied investigations and even fought court orders to preserve evidence, undermining accountability.
- Federalism and states' rights: Washington has essentially threatened Minnesota's officials, saying federal agents "won't be needed" if our governor and mayor simply comply with the White House's hardline immigration demands. This chilling conditionality feels like coercion rather than cooperation.

As an immigrant, I was taught to revere the US Constitution – the very document that ensures no person, not even the president, is above the law. What I see playing out in Minnesota is a direct challenge to that principle. When federal agents can operate as an unchecked force, leaving death in their wake and face minimal scrutiny, it puts all of our freedoms at risk.

Not Just a Minnesota Problem – A National Threat

It would be a mistake to view this as only a local Minneapolis issue. The outrage here is echoed nationally—protests and vigils for Renée Good and Alex Pretti have spread far beyond Minnesota. Americans everywhere are watching to see if our government will correct course or continue down a path of authoritarian-style enforcement—even those who normally champion law-and-order are uneasy. A prominent Minnesota Republican, in an unprecedented move, dropped out of the governor's race and condemned the federal crackdown as "federal retribution on the citizens of our state". When voices on both sides of the aisle raise the alarm, we should pay attention.

From my perspective as someone who chose to become an American, what's happening is more than a policy dispute – it's a moral and constitutional crossroads. I came to the United States seeking freedom and fairness. I never expected to see federal agents patrolling Minnesota's streets as if it were a war zone, nor to see the deaths of innocent people excused and evidence withheld. If this can happen here, in a place as civically engaged and peaceful as Minnesota, it can happen anywhere in America.

My heart aches for the families of Alex Pretti and Renée Good. They deserved far better from the country they called home. We owe it to them—and to ourselves—to confront this national threat. That means demanding accountability for those responsible, insisting on the truth over convenient falsehoods, and reaffirming that our Constitution is not just a piece of paper, but a covenant that binds and protects us all.

As an immigrant, I still believe in America's promise. But belief is not enough; action is required. Minnesotans are standing up right now not only for our neighbors who were killed, but for the soul of our nation. The question is whether the rest of America will stand with us. Our country's character is on the line. The world is watching, and so are we—the newcomers, the citizens, the believers in American ideals. We must not let those ideals be shattered. What is happening in Minnesota is a warning, and we ignore it at our peril. This land of the free must not become a land where freedom dies at the hands of those sworn to defend it.

MICHELLE SHAFFNER

Poet and teacher from Apple Valley, Minnesota

On the Day She Died

Twenty Minutes Away

Bits of paper brindle the sidewalk
where the cracks lay
in between Jersey barriers.
I always look down
as I walk to my car.
There are interesting things
in the school parking lot.

If I look up and see far enough:
there they are 20 minutes away—
homes on 34th and Portland,
families on each side
so much like the one we bought
on 60th and Chicago

so much like the rallying we've done
for what we believe in
so much like my face, my limbs,
my white winter jacket,
driving away to safety

and shot
and headlines
and noise

After We Marched
After He Died

Everything hurts,
and I'm still in the same clothes
because I can't take off
what feels like a hug.

It's cold these days
in Minnesota.
It's cold around these parts,
and this arterial ache,
this jaw crushing in the night,
is a reminder.

And I opened the curtain
to check,
to make sure
the stars are still above.

NATALIE McGUIRE

First generation American

Love always prevails

Minnesota's boundless love has the power to melt even the coldest ice within the deepest hearts, awakening the blind to see with clarity and the deaf to hear the whispers of truth—

truth that Love is all there is.

Now, more than ever, we must come together in unwavering unity and embrace unconditional love for every soul and for our sacred Mother Earth.

Let our hearts ignite with passion and compassion, igniting a movement that will heal, uplift, and transform us all for the greater good of humanity.

NEAL KARLEN

Minnesota author of *This Thing Called Life: Prince's Odyssey On & Off the Record* and *the Tory of Yiddish*

Postcard From the Edge

January 29 at 4:05 PM

I haven't posted on Facebook in a couple/few years--or is it nine months? Who knows, the clocks have been spinning backwards so cuckoo-ly here in Minneapolis that almost nobody I know is quite sure, no jive, what time it is.

Metaphorically, alas, we all know precisely what time it is, and I pray this Old Testament worthy abomination doesn't devolve into 2.5 cable news cycles worth of bobble-headed professional opiners, of all political persuasions, jerking each other off while explaining to us in Minneapolis who we "are" and what this "means."

You're all camera-worthy and smarty-pantsed, no doubt, but please don't move onto Bad Bunny at the Super Bowl as soon as that's a fresher look/ hook.

"Oh thank you, oh Righteous One, for stealing precious seconds away from the barricades to signal your virtue AND—bobble headedly— opine your own damn self," I imagine anybody who might read this saying aloud, with perhaps justifiable snark. I know I probably would.

How odd then, methinks to meself, that I break my FB silence--explained below, nothing noble, and frankly who gives a shit besides me—by posting not stored up profundities, but a Bruce Springsteen song/video.

No, not that one, everybody Not Here I sent THAT (brilliant) song/ video to yesterday afternoon had already seen it, burst into tears, and

97

posted it sans' help from me (and thank you for that, 4real, everyone, everywhere.)

Instead, I'm posting Bruce's 1984 "My Hometown," which I confessed I couldn't stop humming to myself a couple weeks ago to NYC's Joan Feeney—my forever pal/conscience/and caller outer of my own bullshit, who assured me that humming swell songs has been proven by actual scientists to be metabolically helpful.

Never mind that "My Hometown" is a 42-year-old narrative and doesn't really fit the story of what's happening outside my window this moment. I'm no rock critic, thank God, but it delivers, for me at least, the exhausted, palpable DREAD that has settled over, well—my hometown.

NEWELL SEARLE

Minnesota resident and author of the *Alton County Mysteries*

Tyranny Always Wears the Same Face

Tyranny always wears the same face. How can it be otherwise? It begins with a contempt for the decent opinions of mankind. Then tyranny moves on to suborn every institution, law or individual that refuses to submit.

The spontaneous witness of Minneapolis residents on behalf of immigrant neighbors demonstrates our innate belief that persons are created equal with unalienable rights of life, liberty and the pursuit of happiness.

Minnesotans are slow to change their forms of government but are quick to vote and give authorities legitimate power. We have a history of turning out elected officials who treat their office as an entitlement that puts them beyond accountability. It is no surprise that a society that insists on responsible government would take to the streets to protest a train of abuses and usurpations design to cow and submit the city to its absolute control. Under such oppression, it is their right, it is their duty, to oppose as the laws allow these forms of tyranny.

It is ironic that, as we approach the 250th anniversary of the nation's founding, the formal accusation in the Declaration of Independence, modified with contemporary details, still speaks to the present moment of this oppressive Administration. It rings with a clarity that should alarm as well as inspire every Minnesotan and every American.

The history of the present Administration is one of repeated injuries and usurpations, all having the direct object of establishing an absolute tyranny over the states. The tyranny rests on the assertion that the Presidential power is absolute and the President is immune from oversight and restraint. Let these facts speak to a candid world.

He has attempted to render the military independent of and superior to the civil power.

He has attempted to dissolve by fiat, and without Congressional approval and oversight, several departments of the government; usurped the power to determine what kind of history will be interpreted at national parks; fired the governing boards of cultural organizations, demolished one wing of the "people's house," installed himself at their head and put his name on the building.

He has refused to enforce or has reversed measures to equitably accommodate large groups of people for reasons of race, ethnicity, religion, gender or sexual orientation in favor of groups that are straight, white and evangelical.

He has endeavored to prevent the population of the country by obstructing the laws for admitting and naturalizing foreigners; issued orders against admitting immigrants from 70 other countries, especially African, with the exception of white South Africans.

He has located jails and immigration courts at places unusual, uncomfortable, and distant from their attorneys and the depository of their public records for the sole purpose of fatiguing immigrants to leave the country or comply with his measures; for depriving immigrants and legal residents of their right to a trial by jury; and for transporting immigrants beyond seas for pretended offences.

He has repeatedly threatened, sued and indicted local government officials for their refusal to allow local police to engage in oppressing the very people for whom they are sworn to protect.

He has sought for a long time to cause others to be elected on the basis of loyalty to him rather than to the Constitution; he has usurped or suborned the constitutional powers of the Congress and attempted to override legislation with executive orders.

He has obstructed the administration of justice by appointing unqualified federal attorneys and attacked the judges whose rulings and opinions he dislikes; attempted to make judges dependent on his will alone for the tenure of their offices and subverted the aims of justice by pardoning persons who committed heinous crimes against others and the government.

He has excited domestic insurrections amongst us and declared Minneapolis lawless and waging war against it; sent to Minnesota a large army of unaccountable and untrained officers who act with impunity; kept among us, in times of peace, armed troops and militias without the consent and over the objection of our officials and citizens and protected them from trial for the murder and abuse of citizens with mock investigations.

President Trump has used cruelty and perfidy unparalleled in the history of the United States and is totally unworthy as the leader of a civilized nation.

He has withdrawn his support and the participation of the government of existing laws and programs necessary for the public good including USAID, EPA, World Climate Accord and many others.

He has acted in concert with foreign leaders and jurisdictions whose interests and values are contrary to our own; cut off our trade with all parts of the world; imposed tariffs on us without our consent; without Congressional approval sunk or captured the ships of other country on the high seas.

In every stage of these oppressions we have petitioned for redress directly and through the courts but our repeated petitions have been answered only by repeated injury. A President, whose character is thus marked by every act which may define a tyrant, is unfit to be the ruler of a free people.

PAMELA R. FLETCHER

Poet, editor, and Publisher of **Arcata Press | Saint Paul Almanac.**

The Power of Language

We wordsmiths know the power of language. We capitalize on it, exerting, employing and exploiting words to stir our audiences. To craft impactful messages, such intentionality is fundamental. Politicians also know that language can provoke their constituents and others whom they intend to persuade, particularly with the intent of 'othering'. Since January 2026, when U.S. Department of Homeland Security began its Operation Metro Surge to enforce and reform immigration in Minnesota, media outlets across the nation and around the world reported information riddled with descriptions like immigrant scrum, criminal illegal aliens, domestic terrorist, and the worst of the worst, and adjectives like endangered and weaponized.

Prior to January 2026, on January 12, 2018, CNN and other media outlets reported that while discussing immigration policy, Donald Trump had referred to African countries, Haiti, and El Salvador as "shithole countries." On December 12, 2025, he expressed such a sentiment again in referring specifically to Somalia. Weeks earlier, *The New York Times* and other media outlets reported that on December 2, 2025, Trump referred to Somali immigrants as garbage. Is there any wonder that such depictions of the other could cause somebody, a *real* American, who believes what they hear, to "fear for their lives" and to justify state violence?

This *real* American sees the other as the pariah, the kind that looks, speaks, walks, and drives in a certain way. This pariah emigrated or fled from Africa, Asia, Latin America, and the Middle East to escape economic hardship, political oppression and instability, and religious persecution to attain an invulnerable life in the United States of America. They did so just like the inrush of Europeans, who would eventually become "white," who immigrated to the new world between 1820 and 1930 and still immigrate to the USA today, unmolested. Consequently, those of color who are not from the desirable countries of Norway and Sweden, but are from despicable countries, have become indistinguishable from the worst of the worst (e.g., criminals, murderers, and pedophiles) in the mission of Operation Metro Surge. Its apparent aim is to purge the nonwhite pariah from the "Welcoming City" of Minneapolis. This is a test, their first full-frontal attack on American Democracy.

The operators didn't get the memo, though: Don't mess with Minnesota. On January 24, 2026, in honoring the memory of Renee Good and marching peacefully in solidarity to uphold our invaluable democracy, media outlets report that 50 thousand coursed through downtown Minneapolis for the whole world to witness. In stoic Minnesota style, we resisted and rejected federal occupation and retaliation, racial profiling and surveillance via drones and other means, calculated violence, unlawful and forceful entry into folks' homes, illegal arrests and detainments, and indiscriminate use of chemical irritants and projectiles against legal observers, et cetera. Overall, a total violation of Minnesota's sovereignty.

One cold-blooded killing wasn't enough, however. The very next morning, two ICE agents killed Alex Pretti intentionally. It appears that they couldn't stand the peace that had rested on the land for the previous 24 hours. Could it be that they couldn't accept the healing, building, and loving we displayed despite their deliberate chaos? But Renee and Alex didn't die in vain. We will keep honoring their memories. They are fallen patriots, not domestic terrorists. Upholding their sacrifice, we'll keep protecting and striving to retain our freedom across cultural, ethnic, and racial lines. Together.

So, smile, Feds! You're on Candid Camera, seeking to murder bodies and massacre souls, perverting truth, and subverting justice with fallacious words and manipulative imagery. But your evil won't prevail. We're ready and steady with God on our side.

REBECCA SURMONT
Minneapolis, Minnesota

After Effects

It's January cold. The winter of our discontent.
But these are not clichéd times.
Adding to the long list of *unprecedents*
under President Trump
the ground takes the ashes as they are given
canisters roll in streets, spray cans in hands
aimed into faces,
children choke on power; bystanders' eyes burn and beg for milk.
We will share that
people carried milk with their passports,
each for its own protective cover but now
the smell of pepper
wafts on the wind chill,
whistles scream like ominous winter birds.
We find whistles, pop-up style, near sidewalks
and libraries, keep them
in our pockets at the ready.

Tonight, we sang in minus 10 fahrenheit, candles
glowing block by block. Fire pits burning off anger
stoking what peace they could. Their names:
Pretti. Good. An ironic new mantra. New signs
for another march another day. They are dead.
Their killers, free and sanctioned.

Dear Alex

You can rest. We are awake for you
indeed, find it hard to sleep,
the end replayed over and over
like a new Hollywood release.
You didn't want to be famous,
stuck in reels for the world to see.
We toss at night
fighting foreign urges, struggle
for focus, restraint.
Meanwhile you are prepared
for a final rest, all the salutes
aimed back at you. A flag draping.
All the glory.
We ask each other, as you did,
as you reached across the icy slope,
pepper stinging your eyes,
Are you okay?
We aren't. Not yet.

ROB HARDY

Poet Laureate of Northfield, Minnesota 2016-23, and currently chair of the board of the Southeastern Minnesota Arts Council

A Witness

You can be murdered, and the mob
will write your obituary.
The Vice President
will blame you for the bullet.

You wake up this morning,
check the weather,
think about the condition of the roads,
think about all the things that need fixing.
This morning you are
ordinary and unknown.

You just want to raise your child
in a better world.

How easy it will be to conclude
you didn't deserve to live.
How quickly you will become a meme,
followed by a chain of laughing reactions.

For every meme, let there be a poem.
Let every poem be a witness.

This morning the sun rose,
but it never set.
There is still enough light to see.

Grassroots

Enough of this winter.
I just want to go back
to writing about prairies.
I want to think about grass.
The idea of August.
A day innocent of headlines.
Long stanzas of bluestem
and sunlight. Most days now
I don't know what to do.
No warmth from winter's
weakling sun. But I know
the grass holds sunlight
in its roots. In the frozen earth
there are a million sparks.
I have seen the prairie
burned over and rise
from the ashes greener.
Tonight we stand together
on a street corner singing.
Our feet are cold,
but there is warmth in our roots.
With these tiny candles
in this January cold,
we are only grass.
When winter's occupation
is ended, this is what lasts.

ROBERT SAXTON

Resident of Bemidji, Minnesota, and author of *Return of the Manitous*

Hazzards

I found my neighbor's car
In the middle of the street.
Driver's door, open.
Engine, still running.
Coffee, still warm.

In July, I gave him tulips.
He brought me peppers.
I took a bite - too big.
He watched my face turn red,
And laughed until he cried.

When my mother died
He gave me a card,
And held me as I shook.
He kissed me on the cheek.
We talked of family. And the Twins.

At Christmas, he saw my limp
And asked about my knee.
He shoveled my steps,
And brought me groceries.
(And lots more peppers)

I found my neighbor's car
In the middle of the street.
My knee is sore. And I am tired.
But I am getting my coat.
And I am going to war.

SANDRA MAHANIAH

Former resident of Minnesota, now Massachusetts, and author of *Calling the Rain*, an African Memoir (forthcoming)

Is this your first dictatorship?

In a *Daily Show* skit a few months ago, the cast expressed outrage about actions taken by President Trump, until Ronnie Chieng broke in and said, "Please! Is this your first dictatorship?" Ronnie is originally from Malaysia: it is not *his* first dictatorship, nor is it mine. I lived in Zaire under the Mobutu regime for thirteen years, until 1991. What is happening now in the United States and particularly in my old home of Minnesota, makes me remember a time I would prefer to forget.

From the 1970s onward, Mobutu deployed the military in city streets and at roadblocks along main roads, claiming they were there for "security." Their real role, like that of ICE, was intimidation. In practice, that meant stopping vehicles and pedestrians, asking for identity papers or creating imaginary violations and extracting bribes from them. Unlike ICE, they didn't target immigrants or foreigners. If anything, they were more careful with foreigners because they might be under the protection of an important politician. These soldiers hardly ever hauled anyone off to jail, and never shot anyone. They most certainly did not break into homes and haul people away, nor did they take children to detention centers. They were Mobutu's constant reminder to the population about who was in charge. The soldiers themselves just wanted to supplement their income. "Beans" was a euphemism for "bribe," because soldiers often said they needed "beans for the children." You could call it enhanced begging.

On the other hand, Mobutu's regime controlled all the media, which meant at the time radio, television and newspapers—no magazines and of course no internet. No media could criticize any aspect of the government. Television news stories covered whatever Mobutu did that day, where he was traveling, or which city honored him with an adulatory parade. Broadcasts could also include stories of natural disasters and spectacular accidents, but only if newscasters voiced no hint of Government negligence.

Wouldn't Trump love to control the press the way Mobutu did?

Journalists who skirted too close to opposition were warned, and sometimes jailed, usually briefly. If people wanted real news, they listened to France Inter, the BBC, and other foreign radio programs. Protests and demonstrations were banned, and the government brutally suppressed the few that occurred anyway. Sometimes soldiers opened fire on demonstrators, or they were jailed. Still, a family could usually get a relative out with a bribe. This also applied to other crimes, by the way, at least to nonviolent offenses. The people knew the advantages of this type of corruption. This flexibility, they knew, did not exist in the West. If you got arrested for theft in Switzerland or Belgium, you were going to prison. The Zairians were not so sure they wanted quite that much law and order.

In daily life. people made their living as best they could. The government was a major employer, if a stingy one: a high school teacher with a university degree earned $200 a month. Most people engaged in petty commerce full-time or on the side, sent their children to school, and above all, went to church. Kinshasa probably had more churches per square mile than any city on earth. The Catholic Church was still strong, but Protestants came a close second, including some homegrown evangelicals. Many families spent all day Sunday in church. Even regular Catholic and Protestant services lasted at least three hours. At a major bus stop near the largest market, a daily prayer meeting sprang up, where people stopped to sing and pray on the way to work. It grew so large that police had to start diverting traffic around it, but that was one gathering Mobutu's soldiers never broke up. The more people prayed, the less they protested. People adapted because political oppression was all they knew—their country was never a functioning democracy, and they saw no hope for change. In theory, nobody discussed politics, but in private, with people they trusted, they discussed almost nothing else. Everyone knew somebody in the military or in the Security Services. Those contacts, in secret, exercised their influence when they could to help friends and relatives.

Bribery could get you out of political detention, unless you led public opposition to Mobutu's regime or threatened him personally. And even then, sometimes a big enough bribe or outside intervention could save you. A military officer once said to someone I knew, "You do something very bad, we arrest you and wait. If France Inter doesn't say anything? The Belgians don't intervene? The US Embassy doesn't call? We crush you." Bribery and influence are advantages of corruption that no one talks about. If you got arrested in the US or Europe, you were in serious trouble. In Zaire, you were inconvenienced. Yes, people longed for more freedom. After all, nobody likes to be told what to say and live in fear of being extorted, or worse. But in a country like Zaire, people didn't really know what democracy meant. In 1990, when Western powers forced Mobutu to permit a token opposition party, the *Voice of Zaire* asked people on the street what democracy meant, and the responses were revealing. Most of them said, "It means you can say what you want." Very few referred to a system of government. They couldn't imagine it, because they had never seen it.

We in America don't have that excuse. We have seen democracy, but we are in serious danger of throwing it away. Americans are adapting to repression and totalitarianism in ways I saw in Zaire years ago. Those on the right have a completely different perceptions of Renée Good's murder than people on the left, even when watching the same videos. Even those who are not Trump supporters want to believe that our systems are

113

functioning as they should, because the alternative is too frightening. In print media and online, comments show people trying to justify violence by ICE agents: "Well, after all, *those people* are here illegally." When it is clear ICE has snatched a legal resident or U.S. citizen from his home or off the streets: "It was an honest mistake. They let him go later." They refuse to acknowledge that when ICE refuses to look at someone's identity papers, or detains a legal resident or U.S. citizen even for an hour, they are acting illegally. That is the same kind of intimidation Mobutu practiced in Zaire. Many people of color now carry their papers on them wherever they go. On Instagram recently, a man with an African accent filmed himself with his U.S. passport taped to his brown forehead. I'm not sure even that will help. And don't imagine that being white will benefit you: the street murders of two Caucasian Minneapolitans prove that.

Minnesotans standing up to Trump and MAGA and ICE need and deserve our support. I can only hope the rest of us follow their example. We have options that people in other countries don't, and it would be immoral not to use those options. And if we don't, we will continue down the road to fascism. The warning of Martin Niemöller remains as relevant as it was seventy years ago:

> First they came for the Communists
> And I did not speak out
> Because I was not a Communist
> Then they came for the Socialists
> And I did not speak out
> Because I was not a Socialist
> Then they came for the trade unionists
> And I did not speak out
> Because I was not a trade unionist
> Then they came for the Jews

And I did not speak out
Because I was not a Jew
Then they came for me
And there was no one left
To speak out for me.

SARA MENNING

Minnesota poet

child-free woman learns the bus routes in her neighborhood

the streets by my apartment
are named after birds
which ones, I cannot tell you
only that I discovered this recently
learned each road's curves
like wings outstretched
I'd rather be in a park

when I was a kid
anxiety fluttered down my arms
beat into my fingertips
insistent as a whippoorwill
but lately
the dread
has been pecking at my belly
claws scraping through
layers of membrane

walking makes it better
walking makes it worse
I watch my neighbor-kids
flit and hop off the bus
hope they make it home

looking long
into cars parked nearby

many avian species
alert their kin
when danger is near
but some juncos
warblers and finches
point their songs
directly at the predator
waiting to drag them from their nest

SCOTT VETSCH

Carpenter and Minnesota poet

Another Saturday in Minneapolis

It was right around 10 AM when the first text came in that Alex Pretti had been shot and killed. We didn't know his name then but searched the web and found that first video of his death. More videos followed from differing perspectives. Shot in the back by many bullets. The third Federal murder in two weeks.

It was a sub-zero Saturday morning, clear blue sunny sky.

We had been slightly more upbeat that morning, having marched in the huge demonstration that wound through downtown Minneapolis the day before. We joined a General Strike that had shut down our city. The first one since 1934. The company I work for closed its doors.

We had waited for the bus in the cold, wearing our Carhartt coveralls and Sorel boots and the face masks that kept our noses from freezing solid. The bus that stopped was packed to capacity with protestors, heading downtown. The driver told the 8 of us waiting that the bus behind her might have room to take us.

We made it across the river where the entire bus emptied out and walked into the cruel wind. Traffic was stopped, people were open and friendly, chanting. They filled the streets, stopping the traffic, stopping anything normal. We chatted with people we knew. But mostly we didn't know anyone, even in this big city that operates like a small town with that 3 degrees of separation thing going on. But we were together, sharing face masks and hand warmers, staring through the fangs of fascism.

It was the coldest day of the year to date. When we arrived home, our cheeks were wind-burned and our feet were numb, but we felt better than when we left. Love and camaraderie are powerful.

118

But the next morning, sitting in our pajamas, January sun streaming through the windows, the fascist grinch wouldn't let us process even the smallest good feeling. Someone had to die to make their world right again.

It's difficult to make plans during Trump's occupation of Minneapolis. Ironically, we planned to attend a memorial service for a sculpture friend in Wisconsin that afternoon. A woman who died of natural causes. But quickly I realized we would need to attend a memorial gathering for someone much younger. Someone I didn't know, who was brutalized and murdered across the street from a donut shop in the morning sun.

We dressed even warmer this time, jumped on the bus, heading for where Alex was killed. Police cars blocked the road when we got close so that the bus had to turn off route. So, we got off and started walking, angling southwest through the residential blocks. I noticed a case of bottled water poised on the curb, rounded the corner, and there was the intersection.

Hundreds, thousands of people, the intersection was full, thronging, swelling from where the four streets met. An amoebic "X" of outer-wear. Standing room only. In the middle speakers and chanters stood on dumpsters dragged in as a stage. All faces focused. Faces wearing goggles and construction-worker gasmasks, ice frozen on their chests where water was poured into their eyes to combat the tear gas. Ground littered with Pepper spray canisters and rubber bullets.

Border patrol had left the scene. Gone before I arrived. Finished with the brutalizing of this crowd today. They had gone hunting elsewhere.

"These streets our Streets." My favorite chant. In this country there's not much else we own. There's a truth in that. Our taxes build them, fund them. The buildings looming above us with their locked doors are owned by corporations. No right to gather. No public space.

On our streets we are targets. We can be killed with impunity. Drones buzz above my head. If I had a shotgun, I could shoot them out of the sky like geese.

An invasion, a war. It bores me to write this. I want to write about other things. Not wait for the next tragedy. ICE see us as an enemy in our own homes. On our own streets. We are just people. Flawed people. Regular people.

It's January. We're not suiting up to snowshoe or cross-country ski. We suit up to stand at a site where a man was killed.

We have done what we can today. Standing in the cold. Shoulder to shoulder with our neighbors. Using words, not fists.

I want to use my fists. I want to swing back with a stick.

You don't have to swing a stick to die at the hands of these swine. You need only lift a camera to document what is happening in front of you. The masks, the guns, the combat gear. The Nazi haircuts. The derision and contempt.

We walk down the street to warm up. Choose a Jamaican bar, windows steamy, filled with every color of person. Filled with voices, laughter and release. We are suddenly over-dressed beneath our layers. I approach the bar. The bartender is a beautiful, black male, statuesque with shoulder length dreads. I order a round of whiskeys.

"Neat?" He asks. "Obviously." I reply. "No ice."

He tells me he was in the Army for 13 years. Served in Afghanistan and Iraq. Was an MP. Asks me if I can pay. They are subsidizing those who can't. I tell him I am paying. He throws in a beer for free anyway.

"This must have taken you by surprise," I tell him, "Not how you thought this day was gonna go down, half a block from ground zero." He says, "No, man. We've been working on this for months."

This Is how the siege unfolds. Scanning the news. Dreading the next atrocity. Feeling its weight. Days move quickly. Rage flashes at hypocrisy and injustice, at the lawless actions of these green-vested thugs.

We sit together. Family and friends. Shaking off the cold. Telling the stories of our day so far. Debriefing. Every so often the bartender raises a fist in the air, calls out for a cheer and the room responds in unison. I feel better.

STEVEN E. MAYER, PH.D

Author of *My Father Against the Nazis* and *How to Save the World: Evaluating Your Options.* Resident of Amsterdam and Minneapolis.)

Is the US becoming like Germany in the 30s?

"Was Germany in the 1930s anything like the US now?" I get asked that a lot, not because I was there but because my parents were, and my father left behind plenty of papers and correspondence for me to study—which I did recently, along with deep dives into the history of that era.

Basic answer: Yes, there are similarities between then and now, as well as many differences, the most important being that the US has a lot more going for it—historically, culturally, and politically—than Germany in the 1930s.

First, Germany had only fifteen years of experience with democracy from the time it established the Weimar Republic in 1918 until 1933, whereas the US has had almost 250 years of experience with democracy, however clumsy or imperfect it may often seem. When Germany first adopted a constitutional government, it was at a dark time in that nation's history—a defeated emperor with a defeated army, a wrecked economy, and a dispirited population. The first thing Hitler did when he became dictator was to abolish the constitution and the institutions of democratic governance.

Second, German culture embraced authority, especially hierarchical, entitled, and militaristic authority, and had done so for centuries, taking it to higher levels than any other nation in modern history. Americans from the beginning distrusted authority, disrespected it, disobeyed it, thumbed their noses at it while carrying flags, saying, "Don't tread on me," and crossed the forbidding Appalachians to settle lands beyond the reach of The Law. In America, defiance of authority is a way of life, and outlaws are national heroes.

America's strengths have always been our basic rights and freedoms, as guaranteed in the Constitution and its twenty-seven amendments. This is the foundation that makes our country exceptional—and great. This is the self-proclaimed land of the free and the home of the brave, working "to secure the blessings of liberty to ourselves and our posterity." Among these are the Bill of Rights, the first ten amendments to the Constitution that secured freedom of religion, speech, and the press; rights of assembly and petition; the right to bear arms; security against unreasonable searches and seizures; rights in criminal cases, civil cases, and rights to fair trial; as well as the rights guaranteed by the 14th, 15th, and 16th amendments and others that came later. Germany had nothing like that in the 1930s, and Hitler did nothing to encourage it.

However, at the time of this writing, January 2026, there's no doubt that our rights and freedoms are under threat in ways never experienced in this country. In his classic *The Rise and Fall of the Third Reich*, William L. Shirer recounted the three major principles that guided Hitler's journey from convicted and jailed traitor to the top job—"the leader"—in less than ten years.

Propaganda. Rhetoric based in grievance, lies, bogus theories of history that demonize others and glorify racial superiority, seeking retribution, creating crises to assert leadership, smugly luxuriating in violence. "Germany has lost its greatness (losing the First World War) and someone must be blamed. We're better than everyone and deserve more, so we'll take it. Democracy is for losers."

Organizational control. On no one's authority but his own, Hitler rewrote the whole structure of the nation's governance, put himself at the top, and ruled through coercion. With only one legal party, elections were unnecessary. By placing himself above (rather than alongside) the legislative and judicial systems, he controlled everything: the media, the military, the church, the arts, the professions, the schools, the libraries, and proclamations of what's true and what's not. Skullduggery and strongarming the country's aging and weary leadership allowed him the final ascent to the top. The legislature, forcibly deprived of a few rival voters, assented, reducing itself to an advisory role.

Bullying and terror. Behind closed doors Hitler threatened those who disagreed with him. He created his own paramilitary police force (the "stormtroopers" or "brownshirts"), notorious for its brutality, accosting people on the street, beating people, disappearing people, separating families, relocating people to camps for "re-education," and later, escorting them to their death. He militarized the entire nation, sending them to conquer and occupy the entire continent. He and those he commanded were responsible for the deaths of tens of millions.

Many Americans recognize these principles at work even now. And in Minneapolis, where I live, we're seeing and experiencing them up close, in more advanced stages. Many fear we're seeing a trial run of more enlarged efforts to reach for more and more control of a free state by a ruthless central government.

If the United States is to survive as a nation still living, cherishing and defending its original ideals, we must protect our rights and freedoms—protecting them from elimination by arbitrary and vengeful politicians, because once they are lost, they're gone for good. That's what happened in Hitler's Germany.

Former President Clinton told us, on an anniversary of the nation's birthday, "There's nothing wrong with America that can't be fixed with what's right about America." We must protect our democracy from those who would corrupt it—with liberty and justice for all. We must use our constitutional and legal rights and freedoms or we'll lose them.

Use them how? Advocacy and support for organizations and institutions vital for maintaining democracy, such as the ones Hitler destroyed. Advocacy and support for organizations that strengthen our people and cultures at the community level, through housing, safe food and water, creative expression and truth-telling, education and skill development that allow people the prospect of upward mobility. Advocacy and support for organizations that provide emergency food, safety, and shelter, and that try to address the gaps created by inadequate public policy or private practice.

SUSAN JARET McKINSTRY

Poet and teacher living in Northfield, Minnesota.

Thin Ice

Walk onto thin ice and hear the warning crack.
Each step is perilous. Vicious masked thugs
swarm cities and towns, armed and aching for battle.
Their targets: elders, workers, parents,
terrified children, shocked witnesses. Yanked
from cars, jobs, schools, homes, people disappear.
Far away it seems unbelievable. Close up it is unbelievable.

We are all targets. Can you bear it?
Lies echo and repeat, pepper spray and bullets
break American bodies, shred the Constitution.
Our tears freeze as we stand together in protest.
Democracy is shattering. We are all
on thin ice. Minnesotans march and sing.

SUSAN KOEFOD

Resident of Saint Paul, Minnesota and author of
Albert Park: A Memoir in Lies

Mischief

In St. Paul, on Grand Avenue, stands a house,
A playground painted in the colors of pride,
Where Mischief reigns among the toys.
Rainbow banners flutter—affirming life
For every child, each outcast, and every immigrant dream.
Darker winds rattle its shelves
When ICE suddenly appears with audits and silent threats,
Demanding papers--proof of who belongs--
ICE warns the keepers: do not tell a soul.
The shop resists. The phones ring with callers
Seeking to protest with Mischief's toys, posters, and banners.
The local residents gather to "arm" for the streets--
Six free protest whistles are handed to each grownup guest.
The whistles shrilling alerts pierce the ICE-filled streets
Of Minnesota cities, suburbs, small towns, and the tiny hamlets.

We dream of warm sunlit days when ICE's visit is just a bad memory,
When children learn to whistle through blades of grass,
And the sweetest whistles heard in the streets
Are in the calliope melodies of ice cream trucks rolling by.

SUSAN THURSTON

Poet, Minnesotan and author of *Sister of Grendel*

A Good Drop Off – January 7, 2026

Good job, Timmy. We're not late.
Yes, I told his folks. You're set
for a play date on Saturday.
Quick kiss. Sorry, sloppy – I know.
Don't worry, Mommy will keep
your stuffies right here on the dash.
They'll be waiting for you.
Okay. Have a good day, my love.
Be good, kiddo. Learn lots.
Yes. It's pizza night. I'm excited, too.
We'll both be picking you up.

Shoot First

For Renée Nicole Macklin Good, 37

Shoot first. Don't even ask questions
later. By all reports, the woman
with the musical name:

mother, spouse, daughter, sister,
friend, laureled poet. A good observer.
That last one wrenched her from the others.

A man with ice for a heart point-blank
punctuated her last words
That's fine, dude. I'm not mad at you.

To my front deck railing I clip a broadsheet
of the First Amendment. Nestle an eternal flame above it.
Hear another poet whisper, *We murder poets here.* Shoot

TED KING
Jazz Poet and patriot from Minneapolis

Gil Scott Heron Was Wrong

Gil Scott Heron was wrong
The Revolution will indeed be televised

But it won't be shown on your local channels
It will be on PBS, Youtube, and Tik Tok,
And on Netflix with commercial interruptions

The Revolution will be televised
But it won't be called "The Revolution"
It will be called Fake News

The Revolution will be televised
And it will be blamed on Norwegian lefse smugglers

The Revolution will be televised
And top government officials and donors
Will be watching from the underground bunker
Beneath the big beautiful ballroom

The Revolution will be televised
But not on Super Bowl Sunday

The Revolution will be televised
And word on the street is

You can watch it at Johny's Bar
For the usual two drink minimum.

Hey People
The Revolution is being televised right now
The Revolution is being televised right now
The Revolution is being televised right now
The Revolution
Is being televised
Right
Now

TIM NOLAN

Poet and attorney at law, Minneapolis.

Winter—Powderhorn Park

We used to come here for fireworks 4th of July
We spread out a blanket and lounged on the hill
Looking up at those bursting flowers and all
The families all at once would ooh and ahh
Now it's winter the neighborhood is filled with
Parked cars people coming from all over
Climbing over snowbanks along the icy bike path
Creeping down that same hill now slippery
A brass band plays Mexican tunes people carry
Signs thousands of us coming out and we are now
The old ones coming out among this group and more
Than once a young person offers us a hand to get up
And over a small snow ridge the ground is so slippery
An old person could fall this all makes me tear up now
That I am cared for now by these strangers when did we
Become the old people who need some help it must be
Different it must become different that we care for
Everyone that we look out for each other because that's
The only way the world can work we've all come out
For a young woman a mother shot in the cold daylight
Earlier this week she was shot by an ICE guy so casually
Like he was blowing his nose or something he said
"Fucking bitch" after he shot her three times in the face
What twisted path led to this I could fall any time

As we walk toward the gathering the speaker is leading
Chants "Fuck ICE" and "Remember Renee" I'm not used to
Yelling in public but I am now it's good to be in this group
Of not-quite-yet Domestic Terrorists nobody knows where
This will all go my city the city of my entire life is on edge
The streets weirdly quiet but we are making noise here and now
Is it enough to come out probably not but for now what we do
Today tomorrow and again there's always much more to do

The Way It Is

Do you have this sense that it's all falling apart
That despite the gentle snow and radio music
We are on an edge that the President is a crybaby
And a cheat that he's clearly in this for himself
That immigrants are scorned that thugs break
Windows in minivans that the college girl is seized
On the way home to surprise her parents that
She is handcuffed that she is shipped off to Honduras
Where she knows no one that the Somali market
On Lake Street is empty that we've become saps
Babies suckers that the government is not ours
That we must last through years of outrage that
Every day there is another outrage that we sent
Venezuelan men to El Salvador to be tortured
That the Department of Justice seeks revenge
That the Department of Human Services seeks ill health
That the Department of State seeks dominance
The Department of Defense is now the Department of War
That the Navy sends drones to kill fishermen
That every day is another outrage another diversion
We don't know what is happening under cover
The overt acts are criminal the conspiracy is on the front page
That every day is unprecedented
That every act is meant to provoke
That we don't seem to be making it to 250 years
That the patient is failing that the lights are dimming
That we watch we watch everyday outrage upon outrage
We are entering the normal world of outrage that somehow
Without knowing it we have fully become ourselves.

VENUS DeMARS

Musician and resident of Portland Avenue, Minneapolis

The Death of Renée Good

I was drinking my coffee next to our gas fireplace, warming myself, along with our two cats, while waiting to hear from my wife Lynette Reini-Grandell, who had responded to a Signal Group alert request for witnesses to be present at Green Central Elementary School, just two blocks behind our house. Students were exiting buses and being dropped off by parents when ICE vehicles were observed circling the block and so-called officers began surrounding the school.

I'd been awakened by multiple notifications from our ICE alert group, vibrating my phone since 6AM with ICE sightings and warnings throughout our neighborhood. We were into the third day experiencing an increased flood of ICE agents newly sent into our city. I'd gotten up because I couldn't sleep through it anymore. I trusted that Lynette would be safe after she put on her jacket, boots, hat, and took off out the door responding to the school's request.

By 9:35 Lynette had left Green Central School, had begun walking back home after the school announced an all-clear notice, and was told by a passing driver that more ICE incidents were unfolding on Portland Avenue. She turned her attention there and began documenting this new area of concern: multiple ICE vehicles stopped on our street about five houses north from the corner of 34th Street and Portland Avenue. She observed a maroon vehicle stopped a distance ahead of them at an angle parked across the bike lane to the right of Portland between the parking lane and the first of two driving lanes. Other drivers were working their way around the haphazard checkerboard created by ICE vehicles, who were seemingly unwilling to drive around the maroon vehicle ahead of them. As Lynette passed the maroon car, she scanned the houses on either side of Portland, trying to determine why the ICE vehicles had stopped. Up to this point beginning on December 1st, ICE vehicles had often swarmed around a particular house to abduct and detain people they'd decided to focus on. It made sense this may be that kind of situation unfolding again. She was crossing the street to get a better view when she heard three gun shots, and a resulting crash from what turned out to be Renée Good's maroon car hitting parked cars along the left side of Portland Avenue, three doors north of 34th. She and others were videotaping everything as it unfolded, film which is now shown all over the world. You hear Lynette's yelping shock. Then joining in as the woman next to her began loudly yelling "Shame, Shame, Shame" over and over, and "What the fuck have you done?" as ICE agents walked past them.

At 9:40 AM, I got a text from her saying ICE had shot someone outside. At 9:42. I texted "What!?" and scrambled upstairs to get my clothes, jacket, and boots on.

At 9:47 Lynette began a second video documenting the armed blockade ICE officers had made around Renée Good's crashed vehicle, which includes footage of an EMT having to walk a stretcher past because ambulances could not get beyond the multitude of stopped ICE vehicles now extending throughout the 3300 block of Portland Avenue.

By 10:03 I was walking down our front sidewalk towards the corner of 34th and Portland. Lynette called saying she thought the person shot was being taken towards the corner, but she couldn't get past ICE agents who were blocking everyone's way with weapons and chemical spray readied. I told her I was already almost to the corner and needed her to hang up so I could begin taking video on my phone, which she did, and so did I.

The resulting video I took shows the unfolding chaotic display of multiple ICE vehicles with flashing lights blocking all of Portland Avenue beyond crime tape now being placed and monitored by several Minneapolis Police officers who had arrived on the scene. I noted another light-colored ICE vehicle idling just south of the intersection by a few car-lengths beyond the crime tape. (It occurs to me now that this may have been the shooter's vehicle). I also noted two or three other ICE vehicles parked facing east on 34th street just before the intersection with an individual screaming at them saying they had held him away at gunpoint from being able to help assist the victim.

I was still scanning the intersection when I noticed movement kitty-corner from where I was standing; the motion of an EMT performing CPR on someone behind a boulevard snowbank evidently laying on the sidewalk. A second EMT was watching nearby. There were no ambulances anywhere. I realized this must be the person who was shot, and I turned my focus there and kept documenting that until two ambulances finally were able to get past the multitude of ICE vehicles, now seeming to have increased to perhaps twenty or more.

As I documented the CPR being done, I began to realize that they were already dead. My anger was surging as I documented the nearest of the two ambulances which had finally arrived, leaving with the victim but without a siren blaring. That silence confirmed my fears. I relayed that observation to the maybe twenty neighbors now gathered. I kept filming the aftermath for fifteen minutes before I ended that initial documentation. I then talked with a few people from the press who had arrived and were reaching out to me because others who understood I'd been there for some time and had seen quite a lot. I told them what I saw. I talked with one reporter who had a videographer film our interview. I expressed my fear that I believed the shooting victim had not lived.

I kept the video rolling on my phone.

I observed maybe forty or fifty ICE agents, now having exited their stopped vehicles, crowding the entire 3300 block of Portland, standing in full military gear, all wearing masks, helmets, flack jackets, and weapons as if prepared for war. They looked like the platoons I saw on TV of our military during the US invasion of Iraq during Desert Storm, only the "enemy" seemed to me be us, the residents of South Minneapolis: unarmed neighbors blowing whistles, screaming at them, demanding they leave Minnesota, and eventually throwing snowballs as ICE vehicles began to drive past and through the intersection of 34th and Portland after perhaps eight Sheriff's vehicles arrived, and parked going west on 34th between Oakland and Portland, the occupants in uniform all leaving their vehicles and walking into the mix of ICE vehicles, ICE agents on foot, towards what I now realize was Renée Good's crashed car and the parked cars her vehicle had hit, all pushed up onto the boulevard three doors north from the intersection on the east side of Portland Avenue.

I recognized then documented border patrol chief Bovino, who stood in the middle of masked ICE agents, all seeming to survey the taped off intersection. What strikes me now was their arrogance. Their attitude was as if we didn't exist. As if nothing extraordinary had happened at all. As if they were observing trees in a park, rather than a phalanx of screaming, unarmed neighbors who were in disbelief over what had just unfolded.

I saw a pepper ball shot point blank in the face of someone confronting two of the ICE agents who broke from the others and walked to their vehicle parked on 34th. I documented other neighbors assisting that individual who had walked towards me and knelt with pepper irritant in his eyes and all over his face. I continued to document as the two ICE vehicles parked along 34th began to leave through the alley behind our house, and how a growing crowd of neighbors surrounding that vehicle, temporarily stopped it from moving, until the ICE agents within, who had exited the vehicle, set off a canister of teargas to clear them away.

The crowd slowly increased over this time from just a few of us to fifty and growing.

Lynette had finally been able to join me saying she was okay and was going back inside our house, leaving me to finish my documentation, but I had stopped.

What followed over the next days of the week, through Saturday January 10th, was a multitude of interviews with a multitude of news agencies and reporters, both locally, nationally, and internationally including the BBC, the New York Times, NBC, CBS, CNN, Irish radio, the French news, NewsNation, and finally an in-person interview with a reporter and her videographer from a Swedish news agency called Aftonbladet.

Lynette and I had decided immediately that we were in a position of privilege. We realized we could speak towards truth without fear. Something we've always done, since I first came out publicly as a trans-woman in 1988. All we could do was to make ourselves as available as possible to whatever press reached out to us.

Yesterday morning, Saturday January 10th, was when we went live on NewsNation and we first saw the newly released footage taken by the shooter's phone. It was shocking. So clearly demonstrating that there was no life-threating aggression from Renée or her wife Becca. Instead, they'd been trying to deescalate the situation through humor, joking that the ICE agents should "go have some lunch," and Renée saying she wasn't mad at them, seconds before the ICE agent fired three shots through her windshield and side window as she attempted to move around him. His aim was at her head. It was obvious to me that he'd shot out of rage. But rage over what? A joke perhaps? A joke at his perceived expense? Maybe over the fact that they'd not shown fear? Perhaps because they were obviously a couple, with their dog sitting in the back seat? Will we ever really know?

Next the reporting team from Sweden arrived and we welcomed them in. Lynette was first for their interview while I waited. Lynette was calm and specific with her recall. Countered well when they tried to remind her of what our official government statements said about what, in their opinion, had unfolded. That in their assessment Renée was acting as a domestic terrorist, threatening the ICE officer's life, and therefore to blame for her own death.

It was my turn next, and the anger which had propelled me thus far burst out and I wept openly. I wept for the loss of life. I wept for the mental imagery of the CPR I'd documented. I wept at the recall of the new footage from the shooter's phone. I wept for our country. I wept.

At publication the Swedish reporter was kind with the footage they had taken of me and I am grateful for that.

We four, the reporter, her videographer, Lynette, myself, and my friend Joe, who was present and taking photos of our interview, all walked from our house down to the intersection, and across to the memorial, built on the crash site, which, at the time of my writing this reflection, is still there, and is growing with flowers and offerings. As the videographer filmed, the reporter, presenting in Swedish all that had unfolded to the camera, one of the memorial caretakers, who we've come to know as James, came to us saying he'd seen one of our previous broadcast interviews and asked how we were holding up. I said I wasn't holding up well. Not at all. Lynette and I collapsed into his embrace.

We are all strangers; James, who embraced us, the Swedish news crew who interviewed us, Renée Good and her wife Becca, and all the neighborhood folks who flooded out into the cold to witness on the morning of Wednesday, January 7, 2026. This is what community looks like. This is what our Central Minneapolis neighborhood looks like. This is what Minneapolis, St. Paul, our state of Minnesota looks like. We come out to help you shovel your car out of the snow when a blizzard hits. We will rally against injustice, as we did when George Floyd was murdered on May 25, 2020, just a few blocks away. We will stand against a highly militarized presence prepared for war. And we will stand with our neighbors even if we are strangers, armed with whistles, to preserve our democracy, with our love for our country, and perhaps—depending on the weather—snowballs.

WANG PING

Retired professor, poet, and resident of Minneapolis

How to Clear Ice – Ode to Minnesota

It's a long, violent winter. It's been snowing a lot, freezing a lot, thawing then freezing again—back and forth. Snowblowers become useless as the sun melts the snow by day, leaving ankle-deep slush and puddles on streets and driveways. At night, these puddles freeze solid, paving Minnesota with ice that glistens like the Evil Queen's mirror, like an assassin's eye.

It's too dangerous to live like this. We must crush it, clear it, so we can walk outside again, breathe again, laugh again, and live our lives.

The task is daunting. The ice is thick, hard, cruel, and fully armed—immune to law and order. I have nothing but an old, rusty ice pick left in the shed by the previous owner. Is it enough to clear my street?

I'll never know unless I try.

I walk around the ice bank on the sidewalk. It's five feet high, frozen solid, its white fangs extending into the middle of the street. I lift the pick and hurl it against the ice with all my might. It bounces back hard, leaving no mark.

"Fool," a voice laughs somewhere. "How can your tiny icepick fight this entire wall? Just give up. Do what you're told: obey, serve, keep your mouth shut. Don't be a fucking bitch!"

I circle the icy bank again and find a brown spot, smaller than a penny, where the sun has made a dent in the seemingly invincible structure. Under it, the dark earth is visible. And then I hear it: water trickling toward the street gutter. It is the most beautiful sound I've heard all winter. It syncs with the tune I grew up singing in China—the "英特那雄纳尔."

Arise, ye prisoners of starvation!
Arise, ye wretched of the earth!

As a child, I didn't know what the words meant. I just loved the music. It boiled my blood and pushed me toward a tomorrow where everyone has food, clothes, and shelter, where children can go to school without fear or hunger. And where some of the lucky ones can even go to college, without lifetime debts sitting on their backs like mountains.

The trickling means water is running beneath the ice sheet. Running water means the earth has loosened the ice's foundation. That loosened foundation will let me find weak spots, break them open, let the sun shine in, let the water run through, let the ice return to its origin between earth and sky.

I take a deep breath, raise the rusty pick, shout "Hi-ya!", and throw it into the tiny dent—along with my anger, sadness, fear, helplessness, and despair. It pierces the ice, hits the ground, and water rushes out, filling the hole. I lift the pick again, shoulders down, knees bent, core firm—a perfect horse stance for battle. Another hole appears. Still tiny, still insignificant against the giant dam before me. But I keep going. If I can't break it in one strike, I'll try ten. If ten won't do, I'll try a hundred, a thousand, ten thousand—until a canal opens across the dam, until water carries the crushed ice down the street, into the gutter, into the river, into the sea.

Ice water soaks through my boots. My arms ache from hours of lifting and throwing. But now the impossible dam has a trough, narrow and shallow, pale against the blinding hard ice. The singing grows louder under my feet—the singing water, calling its estranged children home to the bosom of their common mother earth, who loves them unconditionally. Life begins with migration—from the cell, from DNA. Life without movement is death.

Ice is water is vapor is sibling is family.

Can today's hard ice imagine itself as gentle water once? Can he face his wife, young and fresh from Philippine, India, East Europe? Can he eat her delicious food with bloodstained hands? Can he hold his chopsticks steady with the same hand that put three bullets into a young mother's face? Does he slap her and call her a "fucking bitch?" Will his hardened heart ever melt and run with blood again?

I breath, eyes on ice, chipping and chopping with my rusty pick at a dam that seems impossible. Yet now a river sings through it, water rushing by, carrying chunks of ice into the gutter, into the river, into the sea.

I know I'm not alone. On every street in Minnesota, households are doing the same—chipping ice, carving ditches to let the water run. First a trickle, then a singing stream, then a tsunami, flowing toward "a better world's in birth!"

This is the Minnesota I discovered during this long, violent winter: kind, caring, tenacious, courageous, united—hearts and souls rooted deep in the earth.

Right before Covid fell upon us, I was banned from the campus, my car was hit and scratched wherever I parked, my clothes, shoes and phones disappeared repeatedly after my yoga sessions. Friends told me the message was clear, and wondered why I wouldn't leave before things got really bad. I couldn't tell them why I stayed, but now I have words:

Minnesota Nice is real, and goes beyond. It's Minnesota Strong, Minnesota Resilience, Minnesota Kind, Minnesota Just, and Minnesota United…the most precious beacon of light during the long night, for the most needed.

My street will be free of ice, maybe not tomorrow, or next week, or next month. But winter will not hold us prisoner forever. The earth is turning around the sun. One day I will walk down the street along the Mississippi, wind and sunlight on my smiling face.

Freedom will taste extra delicious, especially when it's earned by hard work.

WENDY J. MANUEL

Retired ICU/Hospice Chaplain, Northfield, Minnesota

Liberty and Justice for All

"We have to remember freedom is not free,"
—Alex Pretti, November 9, 1988– January 24, 2026

"We have to remember freedom is not free."
"We have to work at it, nurture it, protect it, and even sacrifice for it."
A peaceful man, his life now stolen, speaks over a deceased veteran's body.
His life now stolen.

"We have to work at it, nurture it, protect it, and even sacrifice for it."
10 shots in 5 seconds. His life now stolen.
Alleged law enforcement officers
believing they are immune, kill a peaceful man.

10 shots in 5 seconds. His life now stolen.
May we never forget to demand justice.
No immunity for these alleged officers, unlike pardoned January 6 thugs.
"In this solemn hour we render our honor and our gratitude."

May we never forget to demand justice.
Words spoken by a peaceful man killed, we now honor your sacrifice.
"In this solemn hour we render our honor and our gratitude."
"We have to remember freedom is not free."

WILLIAM SHAKESPEARE

English author, 1563-1616

THE STRANGERS' CASE

This monologue from the Elizabethan play *The Book of Sir Thomas More* (c. 1590s) in Act 2, Scene 4, is a powerful, Shakespeare-attributed plea for empathy toward immigrants. Known as "The Strangers' Case," it depicts Sir Thomas More quelling an anti-immigrant riot by asking the mob to consider themselves refugees. The scene dramatizes "Evil May Day" of 1517, when Londoners rioted against foreign artisans and traders. In the speech, More asks the rioters to imagine the "strangers" (immigrants) with "their babies at their backs" being forced to leave. The play was censored and never performed in Shakespeare's time.

Grant them removed, and grant that this your noise
Hath chid down all the majesty of England;
Imagine that you see the wretched strangers,
Their babies at their backs and their poor luggage,
Plodding to the ports and coasts for transportation,
And that you sit as kings in your desires,
Authority quite silent by your brawl,
And you in ruff of your opinions clothed;
What had you got? I'll tell you: you had taught
How insolence and strong hand should prevail,
How order should be quelled; and by this pattern
Not one of you should live an aged man,
For other ruffians, as their fancies wrought,
With self same hand, self reasons, and self right,

Would shark on you, and men like ravenous fishes
Would feed on one another.

You'll put down strangers,
Kill them, cut their throats, possess their houses,
And lead the majesty of law in lyam
To slip him like a hound; alas, alas, say now the King,
As he is clement if th'offender mourn,
Should so much come too short of your great trespass
As but to banish you, whither would you go?
What country, by the nature of your error,
Should give you harbour? go you to France or Flanders,
To any German province, to Spain or Portugal,
Nay, any where that not adheres to England,

Why, you must needs be strangers: would you be pleased
To find a nation of such barbarous temper,
That, breaking out in hideous violence,
Would not afford you an abode on earth,
Whet their detested knives against your throats,
Spurn you like dogs, and like as if that God
Owed not nor made not you, nor that the claimants
Were not all appropriate to your comforts,
But chartered unto them, what would you think
To be thus used? this is the strangers case;
And this your mountainish inhumanity.

Top: US Representative Ilhan Omar. Middle row: Minneapolis Police Chief Brian O'Hara and Saint Paul Mayor Kaohly Her. Front row: Minneapolis Mayor Jacob Frey, Minnesota Governor Tim Walz, and US Senator Amy Klobuchar.

Illustration by Robin Schwartzman.

ACKNOWLEDGEMENTS

Thanks to all the generous writers who responded to our call to write against a tight deadline and compose potentially the most important work of their lives. Thanks to Cass Dalglish for helping to get the word out into the community. Thanks to those who have donated money to this cause, and to a future historical volume—the child of this one—to be published later by Afton Press. And thanks to the collective voice of all sane Minnesotans, which has earned us a Nobel Prize nomination, forced the Feds to reduce the surge force by 700, and got a little boy released from detention and flown home from Texas. Five-year-old Liam Conejo Ramos and his father were freed from ICE custody after a court order mandated their release. We hope his little light blue hat will find a place in the Smithsonian when this nightmare is over.

Thanks to the talented Robin Schwartzman for her iconic artwork. And thanks especially to my amazing business partner, Gary Lindberg, for his hard work, integrity, and his instant "let's do it" to my wish to undertake this project. Thanks of course to my small but intrepid staff, without whom this anthology could not have been so rapidly published. I'm sorry we couldn't take all the work submitted and I'm sure some slipped through the cracks. All mistakes are mine, and I'm sure there'll be plenty, since this project was such a barnstorm. So—thanks for forgiving me.

–IGL

www.ingramcontent.com/pod-product-compliance
Lightning Source LLC
Chambersburg PA
CBHW030934090426
42737CB00007B/426